Cairo

Front cover: Sultan Hassan Mosque

Right: Lion guard on Kasr El Nil bridge

TOP 10 ATTRACTIONS

The Citadel Heart of the old city (page 37)

Egyptian Museum Repository of the country's national treasures (page 27)

Giza The world-famous Pyramids and Sphinx (page 62)

Feluccas The best way to enjoy the Nile (page 113)

Coptic Museum Home of Christian art (page 51)

Step Pyramid of King Djoser Take a trip to Saqqarah (page 71)

Mosque and Madrasah of Sultan Hassan Mamluk marvel (page 39)

Khan Al Khalili Cairo's famous bazaar (page 44)

Cairo Tower For panoramic views (page 34)

Ibn Tuloan One of the oldest and finest mosques (page 49)

A PERFECT DAY

7.00am   Early start

Fill up with a good breakfast, such as the buffet at the Ramses Hilton (1115 Korneash An Nil) before grabbing a taxi to the Giza Pyramids. Fix a deal for hiring the same taxi and driver all day.

8.00am   World wonder

Be in line to get one of the few daily tickets allowing access inside the Great Pyramid. Marvel at the outside of the pyramids, and visit the Sphinx and the amazingly preserved Solar Boat.

11.30am   Lunch

Get your taxi back to the city centre for lunch at the famous Felfela restaurant on Shari' Hoda Shaarawi, which has been serving delicious Egyptian cuisine for decades. Arrive early to avoid the lunchtime crowds.

1.00pm   Egyptian Museum

Ten minutes' walk from Felfela restaurant is the Egyptian Museum on Tahrir Square (Meadan At Tahrir). Select only the best and go straight to the remarkable Tutankhamun treasures upstairs.

2.30pm   Citadel

Jump back in the taxi and head towards Islamic Cairo for a completely different feel of the city, followed by a stroll through the nearby Muhammad Ali Mosque. The views from the terrace of the Citadel are stunning.

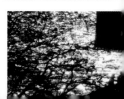

IN CAIRO

5.30pm Sunset sail

Make for the banks of the Nile and bid farewell to your taxi as you swap it for a felucca sail boat on the river at sunset. The noise of the city melts away as you snack and drink, whilst lazily drifting between the islands.

9.00pm Dinner

Floating restaurants such as The Blue Nile or Le Pasha 1901 are moored at Al Gazirah opposite the Nile Hilton. For a truly memorable evening, take dinner whilst sailing up and down the Nile. Even if they stay moored, all offer great night-time views of the city and convert into nightclubs later in the evening.

4.00pm Bazaar

Drop down into the Khan Al Khalili bazaar for some retail therapy. Break the shopping with coffee and cake at the traditional Fishawi cafe, on an alley to the west of Sayyedna Al Hussain Mosque, perhaps accompanied by a smoke on one of the local *sheesha* water pipes.

7.30pm Nile views

Get dropped off at Al Gazirah Island as far downstream (north) as you can, and head to the northern tip of the island. Relax at Sequoia Bar at the northern end of Shari' Abu Al Feda in trendy Zamalik, as the city glistens across the Nile.

CONTENTS

26

15

45

65

54

72

Features

INTRODUCTION

With a population of around 20 million people, Cairo is one of the world's most densely populated cities. Bumper-to-bumper traffic produces a haze above the flat roofs, domes and minarets; its markets are crowded, and houses encroach daily towards the desert. Yet it is a friendly city, full of surprises and easy to negotiate. *Misr*, the Arabic for 'country', is the name for Egypt (officially Jumhuriyat Misr Al Arabiyah, the Arab Republic of Egypt), but the word is also applied to the capital. This is where people from all over the country come to find work.

Last Nile Crossing Point

Strategically located where Europe meets Africa and Asia, Cairo has been a crucial centre for Middle Eastern trade, for Islam and for Near Eastern military power. The city lies at the last fording point of the world's longest river before it wanders off into countless branches in the fertile Nile Delta. From both north and south, all roads and waterways lead here.

Cairo developed from several different towns and communities, which explains the distinct character of its many districts. Its origins stem from the ancient city of Memphis on the west bank of the Nile, from where it expanded into other areas as invaders chose new locations for their capitals. Heliopolis (also known as On) was another early centre 2,000 years ago; the Holy Family supposedly stayed there while fleeing from King Herod. Early Christians developed Old Cairo along the eastern bank of the river, and the Muslim invaders built a new city at Al Fustat. From here, each successive dynasty of Islamic invaders built settlements

The Cairo Tower in Al Gazirah

extending northwards. It was in AD969 that the Fatimid caliph Al Mu'izz declared his new city *Al Qahirah*, 'the victorious', giving Cairo its name.

At the forefront of Islamic culture and development, the city has always been an important centre of learning, claiming to have the world's oldest functioning university, Al Azhar, founded as a *madrasah* in AD988. But the main mosques, minarets and *madrasahs* are largely the work of the Mamluk sultans, who arrived in 1250 and ruled for more than 250 years.

The Expanding City

The city's colonial past can be seen in the handsome 19th- and 20th-century buildings in the centre, on Al Gazirah Island and the opposite banks. Classical streets of grand houses began to radiate from a series of squares and avenues,

Schoolchildren in Cairo, an important centre of learning

and as the Nile was brought under control, the corniche became an elegant esplanade.

Today the infrastructure strains to bursting point, but still the city expands at an alarming rate. Cairo is relentlessly pushing even further into the desert, with new suburbs and satellite towns springing up all the time. Some suburbs are almost cities themselves, and are so self-contained that many inhabitants never venture into Cairo city centre.

1 of the 7 wonders

The Pyramids of Giza are the only one of the Seven Wonders of the Ancient World still intact. One of the others was the Pharos – the Lighthouse at Alexandria, which is now destroyed, but the site can be visited on a day excursion from Cairo.

This is still essentially a desert city, with extremely hot summers and precious little rainfall. Resources are fully stretched. Apart from the Nile and surrounding hills, little is left of the natural landscape as man has adapted the area for his own use. Even the hills surrounding the city are slowly disappearing, as more building materials are relentlessly extracted, covering large areas in fine white dust. Any flora and fauna comes as a surprise, but the recent protection and development of the Al Azhar Park, near the Citadel, is a glorious example of what can be achieved with vision, money and commitment.

Ancient Sites

The Pyramids of Giza come as quite a surprise. Often pictured in what seems ancient isolation, they are in fact on the edge of the city. The line between city and desert, between the last remaining splashes of green and the arid emptiness, is astonishingly stark, quickly realised when arriving by plane. The pyramids are one of the Seven Wonders of the Ancient World, but the real wonder is that such an extraordinary civilisation flourished here for so long. This is why most people come: for the history, for the beautiful tomb paintings, to see Tutankhamun's glittering artefacts in the Egyptian Museum.

Population and Religion

As a commercial and cultural centre, Cairo has attracted communities of Jews, Greeks, Lebanese and many others. Today, Islam dominates daily life, and at the call to prayer, five times a day, people wherever they are, will pull out a carpet and face towards Mecca. Under the Constitution, all legislation must comply with Islamic laws. The Hanafi school of Sunni Islam is the principal discipline, organised through the Ministry of Religious Affairs and controlling the mosques. Some 10 percent of the population is Christian. These are Copts, whose name comes from the classical Arabic word for Egyptians, and most are beholden to the Coptic Orthodox Pope in Alexandria, where there is also a Coptic Catholic Patriarch. A visit to the Coptic area and to the Coptic Museum gives an insight into their rich history.

Naguib Mahfouz

The Nobel Prize-winning writer Naguib Mahfouz was born in a central suburb of Cairo in 1911. The nearby Khan Al Khalili bazaar was the inspiration for many of his favourite characters and locations. As a civil servant in the Ministry of Islamic Affairs, he initially wrote historical novels set in Egypt's past, but in the 1950s he embarked on *Cairo Trilogy*, about everyday life in the narrow streets and alleyways just before Nasser's revolution. His total of 80 novels, short stories and screenplays are not as widely translated as they should be, but they offer a great insight into the family life of ordinary people living in Cairo's crowded neighbourhoods. He died in 2006.

Politically, the country and its capital have led where others have followed. When the charismatic President Nasser brought independence in 1952, it acted as a stimulus for many other countries to shake off colonial control. Within the Arab world, Cairo is seen as the greatest city for education, culture, art, music and media. The silky and rhythmic flow of Cairo's speech cannot be mistaken for any other.

Beyond Cairo

Although Cairo is one of the world's largest cities, it is surprising how quickly one can find quiet rural communities. The pace of life of

The Al Azhar Mosque, symbol of Islamic Cairo

the farming communities below the Saqqarah, Dahshur and Maydum pyramids built along the Nile is still dictated by the seasons, and remains rich in birdlife – egrets, pied kingfishers and herons. Life for some rural *fellaheen* remains much as it did in ancient times, but the sons and daughters of these farmers might well nowadays work in computer centres, tourism companies or medical care.

Tourism

Written guides to Cairo were commonplace a thousand years ago, as religious pilgrims came to look at both Coptic and Islamic sites, particularly the many holy tombs. When

The Nile, 'a gift of God'

Ibn Khaldun, the 14th-century Arab historian, visited Cairo he described it as "the metropolis of the universe...lighted by the moons and stars of erudition." Modern tourism began when Thomas Cook organised his first tour here in 1869. Today the chaotic street life, crowded cafés and traffic jams can cause havoc to itineraries, but they also make Cairo one of the great, enchanting cities of the world.

For some visitors the highlights will be the major sites, for others it is the more personal encounters found in a street market or local coffee shop. There is plenty for the modern tourist to see and appreciate, and the city certainly caters for all tastes. Who cannot fail to be impressed by the pyramids, enthralled by Sufi dancing in the old city or dazzled by the Khan Al Khalili bazaar? And however much you may think you are familiar with the golden treasures of King Tutankhamun, the real thing will still impress.

Over thousands of years, the majestic Nile has flowed serenely through Cairo's heart, bringing life to the diverse Cairene peoples. As Herodotus wrote 2,500 years ago, 'Egypt is a gift of the Nile, and the Nile is a gift of God'. Nowhere is that better seen than in the great city of Cairo, the very heart of Egypt.

A BRIEF HISTORY

Cairo is known as 'The Mother of the World', and human occupation here stretches back to the Stone Age, at a time of ample rainfall. Early man-made tools indicate several villages, particularly in the *wadis* (dry river valleys) close to the modern suburb of Al Ma'adi, to the south of Cairo. As the climate warmed around 5,000 years ago, semi-nomadic wanderers of the Sahara sought a more permanent water supply along the River Nile. With its fertile soil, this region has always been an attractive location for human settlements, and many developed into small city-states that constantly fought each other.

Ancient Beginnings

The main city of Lower Egypt (the Nile Delta) was probably On (ancient Heliopolis), which eventually came under the control of King Menes from Upper Egypt (the Nile Valley). He decided to rule from a new city called Memphis, at a point where the Nile started to split into the many branches of the Delta.

The pharaohs of the early dynasties lived around Memphis, 20km (12 miles) south of Cairo, but there is little to see nowadays as their buildings have been looted or simply disappeared into the Nile mud. But we do have the great legacy of their tombs at Saqqarah, the necropolis of Memphis, where the Step Pyramid of King Djoser is the first stone building in the world. Very quickly this style developed into the true

Funerary mask from Al Isma'ileyyah Museum

pyramid design, giving us the three great pyramids of Giza. The centre of On re-established itself as an important cult centre for sun worship, and the first canal was built from the Nile to the Red Sea around 1850BC. Memphis in the southwest and On in the northeast are the extremities of modern Cairo, which gradually developed between them.

Later dynasties moved their capital further south to Thebes (modern Luxor) and extended the Egyptian Empire, but during times of weakness invaders took revenge, such as in the 7th century BC, when the Assyrians attacked Memphis. Two centuries later the Persians under King Darius I destroyed On, but they saw the benefit of rebuilding the Red Sea Canal.

Alexandria was founded and named after Alexander the Great when he took Egypt in 332BC, and its development took the attention away from the Memphis area. His Greek generals then established their own pharaonic dynasties, known as the Ptolemies, which continued the building of temples and cult worship.

With the arrival of the Romans, a more strategic location was needed to control trade, rather than centres of intellect and worship. A new military fortress was built where the Red Sea Canal entered the Nile and named Babylon, possibly meaning 'Gateway of On'. The spread of Christianity shaped much of what we see today in Old Cairo, essentially what is left of the 'Babylon-in-Egypt' fortress, but the new faith also caused the destruction of many ancient Egyptian temples. It was into this uncertain Christian period that the Persians reappeared, followed by the Arabs, who altered the city for ever.

Arab Conquest

Egypt's first Arab capital was named Al Fustat, taken from *Misr Al Fustat*, meaning 'City of Tents', after the invading General Amr Ibn Al 'ass pitched his tents outside the old

Roman fortress in AD641. To this day, Cairo is known as *Misr* by most Egyptians.

The early years of Islam were dominated by expansion across North Africa, for which Al Fustat was the base. Under the Umayyids of Damascus, Egypt was controlled by a series of governors based at Al Fustat, but things changed with Abbasid rule from Baghdad. The new governor built on fresh land beside Al Fustat, which established the trend of developing a new suburb whenever a new Islamic regime came in.

Baghdad became a great centre of learning, but was a long way from Al Fustat, which languished as a small provincial capital. Abbasid rule initiated the tradition of Turkish war slaves being used as a mercenary army. Usually young boys educated to become loyal bodyguards, these slaves later became known as Mamluks (meaning 'those who are not free'). Over the next thousand years, slave soldiers serving the

The pyramids served as royal burial places

Muslim caliphs gained their own power, some even becoming governors and rulers of Egypt themselves. One such person was Ahmed Ibn Tuloan, son of a Turkish slave from Bukhara in Central Asia, who managed to reduce the amount of taxes paid to Baghdad. With the funds, he established another new centre on a small hill to the north of Al Fustat. All that remains of this area is his Ibn Tuloan Mosque, considered to be one of the greatest Islamic monuments in Cairo.

During the 10th century, the city continued to grow until a new invader came, but this time from the west. The Fatimids, based in Tunisia, took the opportunity of seizing the city from a weak Abbasid governor in AD969, establishing a North African dynasty that lasted over 200 years. Named after Fatima, the daughter of the prophet and wife of the first Imam Ali, these were Shi'a believers. Again a

Shi'a and Sunni

Following the death of the prophet Muhammad, there was a dispute about who should become the head of the Muslim community, known as the *caliph*. Some followers thought that it should be Ali, a cousin and son-in-law of the prophet, but they were outmanoeuvred by those wanting an elected successor, not necessarily related to Muhammad. Ali eventually became the fourth caliph, but was murdered by a rival who stole the caliphate in the name of the Sunni or orthodox sect of Islam. The Sunni believe that the collection of traditions and interpretations known as the *sunna* (path) are as important as the Koran. Since then, the Shi'a (*shi'at Ali*, meaning the 'party of Ali') split away, believing the Koran to be absolute and divine, and started their own lineage of leaders or *Imams*, believing authority should only be through descendants of Muhammad. The Sunni Umayyid caliphate established itself in Damascus, and was later overthrown by the Sunni Abbasids from Baghdad.

new walled city was built, but this time purely for officials, soldiers, servants and slaves. Some of the important landmarks of this new city are still to be seen today – Bab Zowaylah, the main gateway in the south, and Bab Al Futuh in the northern wall. The western wall ran along the old Red Sea canal running up from the Nile, whilst the east faced

Saladin as Sultan of Egypt

the Muqattam Hills. The intellectual and Shi'a heart of the city was the newly created Al Azhar *madrasah*/mosque. Widely acknowledged as the world's oldest university, it is said to have been founded in AD970 by Shi'a scholars from Zebid in Yemen.

The importance of the annual flood cannot be overestimated, as a poor Nile flood could devastate the annual harvest, cause famine and economic ruin, and even topple regimes. Several poor floods one after another weakened the Fatimids, who were unable to help defend Jerusalem and Palestine from the invading Crusaders. The young Ayyubid leader Salah Addin (better known as Saladin) from Syria took the opportunity to push the Fatimids aside and take control himself, as the Sunni branch of Islam was re-established in Cairo. He began a system of *madrasahs* or religious schools, in order to prevent the return of Shi'a influence. He also opened the gates for everyone to come inside and make Cairo the great trading centre that it is today. Most of Salah Addin's efforts were spent regaining Jerusalem and expelling the Crusaders from the Holy Lands, but his greatest legacy for Cairo was the building of the defensive fortress known as the Citadel.

Ayyubid control ended when the sultans could not repel the increasing power of the Mamluks.

Mamluk Period

Based on the island of Al Roadah, the *Bahri* (river) Mamluks took control just in time to defeat the Mongol onslaught, which had already cut a swathe through Baghdad, Damascus and much of Persia and Syria. The success of Sultan Beybars allowed him to develop Cairo as a centre of the Sunni faith, while extending his control to the holy city of Mecca. Under a series of strong successors such as Sultan Qalawoan, more territories were added, and Cairo became a modern capital with hospitals, *madrasahs*, monumental mosques and mausoleums that stand today as the peak of Mamluk architecture.

Under their greatest leader, Nassir Muhammad, the area between the walled city at Bab Zowaylah and the isolated Citadel was urbanised into what we see today, but he always had many rivals to contend with. Emerging from the infighting was a slave by the name of Barquq, who took charge of Egypt in 1382, shifting control to the *Burgi* (tower) Mamluks, based at the Citadel from which they take their name, and also known as Circassian Mamluks because many of them came from the Caucasus region. This was a low point in Cairo's history: murder and bloodshed were everyday occurrences, and non-Muslims were particularly badly treated. The greatest edifice from this time is the mosque of Sultan Mu'ayyad Shaykh, built just inside the Bab Zowaylah.

Towards the end of the 15th century European navigators discovered the sea route around Africa, enabling them to buy spices and exotic goods direct from the Indies rather than from overcharging Egyptian middlemen.

Sultan Al Ghuri, the last Mamluk ruler, was defeated by the Portuguese navy off India and then by the Ottoman Turks in Syria.

Ottoman Turks

The Ottomans, who captured Constantinople, the centre of the Eastern Christian Church, in 1463, took Cairo from the Mamluks 44 years later. As the capital of a province in their mighty empire, Cairo became the flourishing financial hub of the booming coffee industry, which shipped beans up the Red Sea from the port of Mocha in Yemen. Fortunes were made and lost within a few days of the news of a good or poor coffee harvest, before the beans were shipped on to Constantinople and Venice. Other than collecting taxes, Ottoman interference was minimal, as no fewer than 130 pashas governed Cairo, whose inhabitants took little notice of its leadership for almost three centuries. A revolt by the remaining Mamluks at the end of the 18th century created an independent state aimed at improving Egyptians' social and economic status. When the Turks responded, they were

The Citadel, urbanised under Nasir Muhammad

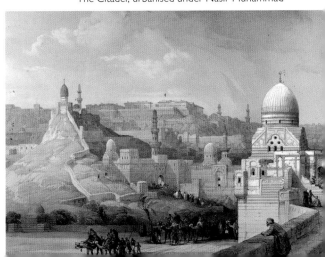

not the only enemy, as the French under Napoleon had also arrived. Unable to fight both, and underestimating French strength, a force of some 40,000 Egyptian irregulars were defeated by hardened French soldiers, and the Mamluks retreated.

Modern Cairo

French control in 1798 brought Egypt and Cairo under European influence for the first time. Modern schools and colleges were built. The rediscovery of ancient Egypt was an important aspect of the invasion. The science of archaeology brought knowledge and understanding of the ancient monuments, most notably after Champollion deciphered the hieroglyphics on the Rosetta Stone. Repeated Ottoman attacks, however, indicated a less than peaceful time ahead for the French, who quickly departed. One of the successful Ottoman

Napoleonic officers in the Tivoli Gardens, Cairo

generals was an Albanian by the name of Muhammad Ali, who promoted himself to governor and ultimately became the great moderniser of Cairo. His first success was to defeat a British force in 1807, and shortly afterwards he decided to get rid of the interfering Mamluks once and for all in a carefully orchestrated massacre, after which around 3,000 further Mamluk supporters were killed on the city's streets.

Mamluk Massacre

Muhammad Ali invited 400 Mamluks to a banquet at the Citadel, where he famously had them well fed and requested them to leave by the lower gates opposite the Mosque and Madrasah of Sultan Hassan. At the last moment the gates were slammed shut and all the Mamluk leaders were murdered.

Muhammad Ali knew how much the Ottoman Turks lagged behind the industrialised European superpowers, and he surrounded himself with French advisers. Under his leadership, Egypt's agriculture and cotton industry was transformed and a new Cairo was built in the marshy area around Al Azbakeyyah and Bulaq, with avenues and squares driven through the old town, destroying much of the city's character and giving it a more European look. His showcase mosque, however, was built on a terrace inside the Citadel, in such a position that it could be seen from anywhere in the city.

His descendant Khedive (Sovereign) Ismail oversaw the building of the Suez Canal, Nile barrages, new railways and the wish to turn Cairo into 'Paris by the Nile'. But Britain and France were envious of this success and soon engineered the country's bankruptcy, giving Britain an excuse to take over the Suez Canal and invade in 1882, turning the Khedive into a puppet ruler of the British. Cairo was the strategic base for the British army when repelling the Germans and Italians invading along the North African coast during World War II.

Since Independence

The last descendant of Muhammad Ali, King Farouk, was deposed when the British were ousted in the military coup of 1952 following popular demonstrations and riots. On becoming president, Gamal Abdul Nasser nationalised the Suez Canal, which was still controlled by the British. An ill-fated British, French and Israeli attempt to seize the canal caused the Suez Crisis in 1956, which ended in failure.

The Six-Day War in 1967 was a major conflict between Israel and Egypt, which was to some extent resolved in the Camp David Peace Accord with Israel by Nasser's suc-

President Nasser with King Saud of Saudi Arabia

cessor, Anwar Sadat. However, Sadat's dealings with Israel made him enemies and he was assassinated during a military parade in 1981.

Sadat's vice-president, Hosni Mubarak, assumed leadership, and negotiated Egypt through the complexities of Middle Eastern politics for 31 years. Demonstrations erupted in Tahrir Square (Meadan At Tahrir) as part of the 'Arab Spring' uprising early in 2011. Mubarak's minor cabinet reshuffles failed to satisfy the public, who forced him from office when the army eventually backed the demonstrators. Hundreds have been killed in violent clashes and the outcome is unclear, as the process of free elections and the formation of a new government continues.

Historical Landmarks

c.3100BC Upper and Lower Egypt unifies, with capital at Memphis.

c.2600BC World's first stone structure built at Saqqarah, known as the Step Pyramid of King Djoser.

c.2500BC Pyramids of Giza constructed by three generations of pharaohs of the 4th dynasty.

332BC Alexander the Great takes Egypt; Memphis loses power.

332–30BC Descendants of Alexander establish their own pharaonic line known as the Ptolemies.

30BC Upon the death of Cleopatra, Romans add Egypt to their trading empire and build the fortress at Babylon.

AD2 The Holy Family flee to Heliopolis and seek safety in Babylon (Old Cairo) area.

1st century AD Christianity brought to Egypt by St Mark; early Coptic churches established.

641 Arab invaders under Amr Ibn Al 'ass bring Islam to Cairo, creating their capital at Al Fustat.

969 The Fatimids seize Cairo, install Shi'a Islamic control for two centuries and establish Al Azhar university.

1171 Salah Addin (Saladin) restores Sunni control. Builds Citadel fortress.

1250 Mamluks extend empire and build great religious monuments.

1517 Start of Ottoman Turkish control. Cairo flourishes.

1798 Napoleon's troops take Cairo and bring European influences.

1805 Muhammad Ali begins a family dynasty that sets about modernising the city and opens the Suez Canal.

1952 The revolution removes King Farouk and new President Gamal Abdul Nasser declares Egypt a republic.

1981 President Anwar Sadat assassinated in Cairo; Hosni Mubarak becomes president.

2011 'Arab Spring' protests in Tahrir Square against President Mubarak, who resigns and is arrested on corruption charges.

2012 The process of free elections and the creation of a new government continues.

WHERE TO GO

GETTING AROUND

The first thing to realise about the city is that traffic is heavy and unforgiving. Just crossing main roads can be a major undertaking for the pedestrian. But taxis are easily had and inexpensive, and the limited metro system is simple to navigate. The centre of the old city, with narrow lanes, is fun to explore, and perhaps get a little lost in, while the Nile and the Cairo Tower provide constant points of orientation.

CENTRAL CAIRO

The animated heart of central Cairo **is Tahrir Square ❶** (Meadan At Tahrir, meaning 'Liberation Square'), developed in the mid-19th century, and now served by the Sadat metro station. Through 2011 it was the focus of anti-government demonstrations that ousted President Mubarak from power. The low red building at the northern end is the **Egyptian Museum ❷**, one of the great museums of the world.

Egyptian Museum

This is a world-class collection of wonderful artefacts from Egypt's ancient civilisation (daily 9am–6pm; charge; no cameras). But it is also a chaotic, crowded place, where even the room numbering is confusing. There are so many objects on display that some can only be glimpsed while passing at a brisk pace between the major attractions. Poor labelling and bad lighting mean that a guide is useful to explain things, but equally it is rewarding simply to wander around and look

Muhammad Ali Mosque in the Citadel

Mask of Tutankhamun

at whatever takes your interest. Such is the draw of the best-known exhibits that while groups crowd some rooms to bursting point, others remain empty.

On the ground floor, the objects are placed in roughly chronological order, going clockwise around the outer rooms and corridors. The central area is dedicated to the 18th-dynasty Amarna period, especially the remarkable remains of a painted plaster pavement, showing Nile River scenes with fish and ducks. While climbing the steps to the first floor, and the justly famous Tutankhamun treasures, look out for the wonderful display of ancient papyri on the staircase walls, still with remarkably fresh colours. Objects found in the boy king's tomb take up two of the four sides of the upper floor and include the stunning gold death mask, the two innermost golden anthropoid coffins, jewellery, wooden shrines, chariots, beds and footwear. The thousands of items in the corridor include his magnificent golden chair and footrest, plus two life-size guardian statues.

Just behind these is the entrance to the Mummy Room (additional fee), displaying the skills of the mummification process on the bodies of some royal rulers, including Seti I and Rameses II. Nearby is Room 53 (no extra fee), which displays mummified animals considered sacred to the ancient Egyptians; it is fascinating to recognise animals such as gazelles, snakes and baboons wrapped up for eternity.

Other rooms not to be missed include The Royal Tombs of Tanis, Ancient Egyptian Jewellery, and the beautiful paintings and statues in Room 32 (downstairs).

A new museum, the Grand Egyptian Museum, is being constructed close to the Pyramids, to provide additional capacity in a modern, more secure setting. Once that is completed in 2013, artefacts will be redistributed between the two museums.

Downtown

At the opposite end of Tahrir Square is the towering Mugamma'a Building, housing government offices. Just to the east are the pleasant grounds of the downtown campus of the **American University in Cairo** (AUC), established in 1919 in what was an old ministerial building. Security is tight to reach the bookshop, galleries and lecture theatres, which are usually open to the public.

One block south from here along Shari'a Al Qasr Al 'Eani is another set of government buildings including the parliament, identified as the Shoura Council. It is usually possible to visit the **Ethnographic Museum** and the **Geographical Society of Egypt**, housed

The Egyptian Museum

in the same building (Sat–Wed 10am–3pm; free; no cameras). That said, the security guards are not that happy about allowing this, and require visitors to leave their passport or ID card at the guardhouse. The ground floor is a dusty collection of everyday items covering hundreds of years of life in Cairo. An African room of spears and elephant tusks gives a flavour for the Geographical Society located on the first floor, centred on a beautiful wooden lecture theatre and reading rooms. The Suez Canal Room has a series of models showing the course of the canal through lakes and cuttings, with an extensive selection of old photos and prints.

Any of the streets running east from here through the Bab Al Luq' area lead to the **Abdin Palace** ❸, a residence for Khedive Ismail built in 1872. Access to the **Abdin Palace Museum** (Sat–Thur 9am–3pm; charge; camera fee) is from Shari' Mustafa Abd Al Raziq running along

Al Azbakeyyah Gardens, with a statue of Viceroy Ibrahim Pasha

the rear or eastern walls. The museum is full of ceremonial swords, guns and official gifts such as a gold-plated automatic weapon from Iraq. Other rooms contain an impressive collection of medals, silverware, an array of medieval arms and an amazing armoured breastplate with 19 fixed gun barrels pointing in all directions, apparently operated by a lever system.

The Tiring Building, just north of Meadan Al'Atabah

As the modern downtown developed to the west of the medieval city, a transition zone between the two was established, running from the Abdin Palace northwards to the new railway station at Rameses Square (Meadan Ramssis). The grand **Al Azbakeyyah Gardens** ❹ were laid out beside Atabah Square (Meadan Al'Atabah), which became the focal point of ancient and modern, east and west. A new opera house fashioned on La Scala in Milan was built, as well as lavish hotels such as the original Shepheard's and the Continental. Grand residences, coffee shops, restaurants and sumptuous new food and department stores catered for the wealthy inhabitants.

Just north of Atabah Square along Shari' Al Musski is the architecturally famous **Sednoui Building**, named after the Syrian village birthplace of the two brother owners. The equestrian statue in the centre of Al Azbakeyyah Gardens is of Viceroy Ibrahim Pasha (1789–1848). This central position was also chosen for the main fire station and post office. The **Post Office Museum** (Sat–Thur 9am–1pm; charge) shows the carrying of messages from pharaonic times (there are famous statues of scribes) using horses, carrier pigeons and air mail, as well as postboxes, uniforms and, of course, plenty of beautiful stamps.

To the north of Al Azbakeyyah Gardens all roads lead to Meadan Ramssis, a great intersection of highways, flyovers, metro lines, and bus and taxi routes. Every few years the planners change the layout, but it's always a chaotic place full of people on the move. The major railway station of the country is here, with a useful tourist office for arriving passengers. The attached **Railway Museum** (Tue–Sun 8am–2pm; charge) has a couple of old locomotives and a fantastic selection of Art Deco posters. Upkeep is minimal, so unfortunately most of the dusty railway layouts and models look as though they have been depicted during earthquakes or rail disasters.

The **Korneash An Nil ❺** (Corniche) is the name given to the busy main road running along the eastern bank of the river; a walk beside the Nile is especially pleasant late in the day, when felucca sails can be seen silhouetted against the setting sun.

Tiring Building

The Sednoui Building is not the only famous department store around Atabah. Usually seen when zooming along the Al Azhar flyover from Al Azbakeyyah Gardens, the neglected Tiring Building, just north of Meadan Al'Atabah, was the first large department store in Cairo. Named after Austrian owner Victor Tiring and designed by architect Oscar Horowitz, it was built in 1913 for the wealthy new European area around Al Azbakeyyah Gardens. Its globe glass dome, supported by four figures of Atlas, which once shone brightly at night, is now shattered and painted over, but it briefly regained fame in 1997 as the centrepiece in the Egyptian film Al Tofaha.

Smart address, Al Gazirah

Al Gazirah

Immediately opposite the downtown area is the southern end of Al Gazirah, dominated by the Cairo Tower. The 6th of October Bridge (Kubri Sittah Octuber) crosses high above the island, giving good views of the Gazirah Sporting Club, but the more southerly Tahrir Bridge (Kubri At Tahrir) accesses more sights beyond the statue of former prime minister Sa'd Zaghlul. Immediately to the right are the well-kept Andalusian Gardens running beside the Nile, which also contain an obelisk from a temple at Tanis in the Delta.

Gates behind the Sa'd Zaghlul statue lead into the extensive area of the **Opera House Complex ❻**, which has been redeveloped as a cultural centre on the old Cairo Exhibition Grounds. The elegant Opera House itself was opened in 1988 to host opera, ballet, jazz, classical and Arabic music (see page 89). The nearby **Museum of Modern Egyptian Art** (Tue–Sun 10am–1pm and 5–9pm, Fri 10am–noon;

charge) has a permanent collection of contemporary paint-ings and sculpture spread over three floors, as well as tem-porary exhibitions. There are other art centres and a music library on the same site.

Across the road from the western entrance (behind the closed planetarium) is the **Mokhtar Museum** ❼ (Tue–Sun 10am–1pm and 3–5pm; charge; no cameras), dedicated to the work of the country's greatest sculptor, Mahmoud Mokhtar (1891–1934). Smaller exhibits and models are inside, with others outside, but the largest pieces are to be seen around the city. Just up the road, the Sa' statue is one of his, as is his giant sphinx and goddess entitled *Egypt's Awakening* on Al Gama'a Square (Meadan Al Gama'a) at the entrance of the university and zoo.

The **Cairo Tower** ❽ (daily 9am–noon; charge) has been a feature of the Cairo skyline for half a century, and provides

Cairo Tower

wonderful panoramic views of the city. These are best on a windy day, when pollution is blown away, but queues can be long to access the tiny lift.

On the northern half of the island, the vast open space of the **Gazirah Sporting Club** was an exclusive members-only club during British control and still has horse-racing, golf, tennis and other sporting activities. The northern tip of Al Gazirah is a tightly packed area of embassies and luxury accommodation known as **Zamalik**.

Art Deco Mansions

Fronting the Nile on the eastern side of Zamalik are some stunning Art Deco mansions. Built during the 1930s, with names such as Pyramid House, Nile View and Soliman House, their original exteriors have been preserved, but most of the interiors have been thoroughly modernised.

On the semicircular road running around the outside of the Gazirah Sporting Club is the impressive **Gazirah Arts Centre** (Sat–Thur 10am–1.30pm and 5–9pm; charge; no cameras), occupying the former palace of a cousin of King Farouk, built in 1920. Today it houses the Islamic Ceramics Museum, but it is the magnificent rooms themselves, with intricate carved walls and decorated fireplaces, which are the highlights. Rooms are dedicated to Fatimid, Turkish and Persian periods, and display a range of ceramics and finely carved pottery, such as water filters depicting camels, horses and peacocks. There is even an example of an early pottery hand-grenade! Downstairs are galleries for contemporary art exhibitions, while the rear garden displays modern sculptures.

Just north of the 6th of October Bridge (Kubri Sittah Octuber) is a flotilla of floating restaurants overlooked by some fine **Art Deco mansions** and the Marriott Hotel, developed around the remains of the Khedive's Gazirah Palace, built for the grand opening of the Suez Canal in 1869.

North of 26th of July Bridge (Kubri Sittah wa 'Shrin Yulyu), along the eastern bank, is a string of splendid mansions, mostly occupied by foreign embassies, but there is one that can be visited. The **Greater Cairo Library** (Sun–Thur 9am–5pm; free; no cameras) is located in the former palace of a daughter of Sultan Hussein Kamel, who ruled Egypt 1914–17. Access for casual visitors is around the back to the right, where a passport or ID must be left at the gatehouse. It is very much a working environment, with rooms for study, but the refurbishment has been handled well and offers fine views across the river.

EASTERN (ISLAMIC) CAIRO

The Islamic heart of Cairo is the result of Fatimid expansion in the 10th century, although the most dominant feature is the later Citadel, begun by Salah Addin in response to the

Courtyard of the Muhammad Ali Mosque

threat of the Crusaders. Over the following two centuries, trade allowed the city to expand further, with each new ruler adding to this secular and religious mix, creating today's labyrinth of monumental buildings and crowded arteries.

Citadel

Art Deco building, Zamalik

Aloof from the crowds of people and traffic is the magnificent **Citadel**  (Al Qal'ah; daily 8am–5pm; charge), which has stood guard for almost 1,000 years. Buildings have been added and altered to create a strange mixture of styles, sizes and uses. The open terrace gives the first impressive view of the soaring thin minarets and silver half domes of **Muhammad Ali Mosque**, begun in 1824 by the Egyptian leader Muhammad Ali, who came from Macedonia. Entry is via the open courtyard with an ornate canopied ablution fountain in its centre. The broken clock tower was given by French king Louis-Philippe in 1846 in exchange for the obelisk now at Place de la Concorde in Paris.

The mosque interior is dominated by a multitude of hanging lamps arranged in concentric circles, but try to look beyond them to see some of the beautiful decoration of the upper walls and supporting half-domes. Almost unseen is the mausoleum of Muhammad Ali himself, to the right of the doorway, but nobody could miss the golden *minbar* (pulpit) straight ahead. At the mosque exit, walk along the terrace for spectacular views over the Sultan Hassan and Ar Rifa'i mosques. Several well-known landmarks can also be spotted, including the Cairo Tower, Ramses Hilton and even the Giza

Pyramids if the haze allows. The neighbouring **Gawharah Palace** was once used to accommodate guests and now houses a collection of paintings and dusty furniture.

To the north of the Muhammad Ali Mosque is another terrace leading to the **Police National Museum**, an odd but interesting collection of guns, weapons and police badges. Opposite this is the oldest building to survive inside the Citadel, the wonderful **An Nassir Mosque** from 1335. Inside the prayer hall is an exquisite octagonal carved wooden ceiling, in one of the most tranquil places in Cairo.

The northern enclosure contains the **National Military Museum,** set behind a courtyard full of warplanes and tanks. Inside is a mass of military memorabilia and historical weapons, from ancient times to the present day. The nearby **Carriage Museum** offers eight horse-drawn carriages, but the best part is the **Sulieman Pasha Mosque**. This intimate

Sultan Hassan Mosque and madrasah

building from 1528 is the first Ottoman-style mosque in Egypt. The interior dome decorations are superb, with Persian-style receding diamond motifs in red, blue and white floral designs. The massive towers at the end of the compound can be climbed for great views over Al Azhar Park.

Sultan Hassan Madrasah and Ar Rifa'i Mosque

In the Meadan Salah Addin below the Citadel are two of the most famous mosques in the city, facing each other across a narrow street. Stepping inside the **Sultan Hassan Madrasah** ❿ (daily 8am–5pm; charge) is like entering a formidable Crusader castle, with sharp-angled passageways and dark towering walls. But inside the bright courtyard, the detail is delicate on the four high-arched entranceways known as *iwans*. Each of these is dedicated to a different school of Sunni teaching (a *madrasah* is a Koranic school). The gold-decorated *qibla* wall (indicating the direction of Mecca) and *minbar* are beautiful examples of 14th-century Mamluk architecture. In particular, the *mihrab* (prayer niche) has fine marble work in red, white, yellow and black. Cunningly placed behind the *qibla* wall is the stone tomb and massive mausoleum of Sultan Hassan, ensuring that worshippers are also always praying towards him.

Across the street is the **Ar Rifa'i Mosque** (daily 8am–5pm; charge), built some 500 years later in Mamluk Revival style, along more European lines. It is a pilgrimage spot for worshipping Shaykh Ali Ar Rifa'i, the saintly head of an Order of Sufi dervishes. Inside on the left are four later tombs

Sultan Mu'ayyad Shaykh Mosque from the Bab Zowaylah

belonging to King Farouk, King Fuad, his mother and the late Shah of Iran, who fled here after Iran's Islamic Revolution in 1979.

Just down Shari' As Salibah, which runs west away from Meadan Salah Addin, is the beautifully restored **Sabil kuttub (well/Koranic school) of Qayetbay**, dating from 1479. The milky-blue water in the cistern below is accessed by spiral steps, whilst upstairs you'll find a study, a library and a fine view from the roof.

North to Bab Zowaylah

North of the citadel, Shari' Ad Darb Al Ahmar runs up towards Bab Zowaylah and passes through an area recently redeveloped by the Aga Khan Foundation, including the Khayrbek mosque complex. Beyond that, the **Blue Mosque** (Mosque of Amir Aqasunqur) is in quite a dilapidated state, but there are great views towards the Citadel from the top of the minaret. Further down the street and across the road is the **Al Maridani Mosque** (free; remove shoes). This is a regular, everyday 14th-century mosque, only partially restored, with junk piled in gloomy corners, but it has a beautiful open courtyard full of trees and birds. Alongside the fountain (which was 'borrowed' from the Sultan Hassan Mosque) a few old men pass their lives away, chatting and watching, in an oasis of calm.

Dive into any of the narrow alleyways to see timeless Cairo at work. Woodcarvers and upholsterers create and supply goods as they have done for centuries. Buying an inlaid box direct from the workmen shows just how much the shopkeepers in the bazaar add on. The raised area to the east is part of the Al Azhar Park, but the only entrance is along the Shari' Salah Salim expressway, on the other side.

About 400m/yds to the west of Bab Zowaylah at Meadan Ahmad Mahir is the recently renovated **Museum of Islamic Art** ⑪ (daily 9am–3pm; charge). It houses more than 100,000 objects of fabulous ceramics, carpets, glass, metal and woodwork, and is one of the best in the world. The main section of the museum houses pieces covering the entire Islamic history of Cairo. Especially valuable are those unearthed from the ruined Al Fustat area – Cairo's earliest Islamic settlement. Other sections show Islamic art, such as manuscripts, calligraphy and coins from other Muslim countries. The Egyptian Library next door is not open to visitors.

The imposing medieval city gate known as the **Bab Zowaylah** ⑫ (daily 8am–5pm; charge) is the last remaining southern gate from the walls of Fatimid Cairo, with the locally named **Qasabah** (High Street) running 1.5km (1 mile) north to the Bab Al Futuh. Each wooden door of the gate weighs 4 tonnes.

The towering minarets actually belong to the Sultan Mu'ayyad Shaykh Mosque next door. The gate was such a popular subject for European artists over the last 150 years that their paintings have more recently been used for reference to help modern

David Roberts

Many mosques and well-known ancient Cairo sites were drawn and painted by the prolific Edinburgh-born artist David Roberts (1796–1864) during his oriental travels in 1838. He produced six folio volumes of 247 lithographs of Egypt, Nubia and the Holy Land.

Al Azhar Park

conservators. Inside the gateway on the right is the restored *Sabil kuttub* of Nafisa Bayda. To the left is the red-and-white-striped **Sultan Mu'ayyad Shaykh Mosque** with its fabulously carved bronze doors, which originally came from the Sultan Hassan Mosque and have an interlaced glazed tile-work surround. The narrow spiral steps inside the minarets can be climbed from the top of Bab Zowaylah. The views of the neighbourhood, local mosques and Citadel are well worth the effort.

Along Shari' Al Azhar

Where the Qasabah meets the Shari' Al Azhar are the giant buildings associated with Sultan Al Ghuri, one of the last Mamluk rulers, who displayed his wealth by building on Cairo's most prestigious street. On the left is the 1503 **Al Ghuri Mosque/Madrasah** ⑬ (free; remove shoes), part of the complex which was supposed to contain his tomb, but his body was never returned after he died fighting the Ottomans near Aleppo in Syria. The open courtyard of the mosque has several circular-shaped flooring slabs of green-and-red marble, and four large *iwans* (vaulted, open-ended halls), illuminated by lamps suspended from the ceiling. Below the mosque are some covered alleyways of silk and fabric merchants, who have traded here for centuries.

Before crossing Shari' Al Azhar, turn right for 100m/yds to the **Wekalat Al Ghuri** (daily 9am–3pm; charge), originally a large, five-storey *khan* or trading centre for merchants, now an artistic centre. The central covered courtyard with protruding wooden *mashrabiyas* is used for music concerts and folk groups, in particular the twice-weekly performances of the Tannura Group (Wed and Sat 8pm; free), who perform hypnotic **Sufi dancing** with live music and singing.

Further down this same street, on the left is the **Al Azhar Mosque ⑭** (daily 8am–6pm, except prayer times; free) the first mosque built by the Fatimids, in AD972. The bright courtyard is surrounded by ziggurat-topped arches, supported by single, double and triple columns and dominated by three minarets and a dome. A forest of columns inside the prayer hall leads to the delicate geometrical designs inside the *mihrab* recess. The main gateway is known as the Barber's Gate, where students had their heads shaved before entering the attached **Al Azhar University**. Acknowledged as the world's oldest university, dating from AD988, most of the infrastructure came from an earlier centre of learning at Zebid in Yemen.

Sufism

Sufism is a spiritual path for individual Muslims to follow as they search for the mystical divine. The most impressive method is by spinning around until a trance-like state is achieved, sometimes called a 'whirling dervish'. The Arabic word *suf* means wool, so a Sufi is literally a 'man of wool'.

Bayt As Sehaimi

At the rear of the Al Azhar Mosque is the **Bayt Zainab Khatun** (daily 9am–5pm; charge), a 15th-century Mamluk-style house complete with courtyard and grand reception hall. It is unfurnished, and the best reason to visit is for the magnificent views across Al Azhar from the roof of the property.

East of here is the 30-hectare (75-acre) **Al Azhar Park** ⑮ (daily 10am–midnight; charge; www.alazharpark.com), a welcome new addition for relaxation inside the city. Accessed from the Shari' Salah Salim expressway, it has been developed by the Aga Khan Foundation as a catalyst to improve the general lifestyle of Cairo's inhabitants. The graceful water channels and pools, meandering walkways and cafés are a peaceful and rubbish-free retreat, offering great views over the city. Not surprisingly, the restaurants and cafés, which stay open late into the evening, are extremely popular.

Khan Al Khalili Bazaar to Bab Al Futuh

Returning to the Qasabah, use the footbridge to cross the busy Shari' Al Azhar and enter the bustling centre of the **Khan Al Khalili bazaar** ⑯. Named after one of Sultan Barquq's attendants called Khalili, who dug up the old Fatimid cemetery and replaced it with many *khans* or warehouses for goods, this is what much of Cairo looked like for centuries. With its spices, gold and perfume, it still has an exotic atmosphere, but the narrow alleys can become crammed with tour groups. Apart from the shops, there are several points of interest inside the bazaar, including alleys that became famous in the novels of Naguib Mahfouz and the Fishawi café, a traditional coffee shop.

At the eastern edge of the Khan Al Khalili is the **Sayyedna Al Hussain Mosque**  (free; remove shoes), which has a silver-grilled shrine containing the head of the prophet's grandson, a place of pilgrimage for Shi'a Muslims. The shrine, *minbar* and *mihrab* are all beautifully decorated in tiny blue, red, yellow and white *zillij* tilework. The rooftop restaurant of the Hussain Hotel has great views over the square in front of the mosque. The street running along the mosque's western wall goes to the northern Bab An Nassr gateway.

Further up the Qasabah, at a bend on the right, is the 1820 **Sabil kuttub of Muhammad Ali,** with a fine decorated facade of carved marble and an intricate wooden canopy. From here to the Bab Al Futuh are several more interesting Islamic monuments, including the adjoining

The atmospheric Khan Al Khalili bazaar

In the Southern Cemetery

mosque complexes of Sultan Qalawoan, An Nasir Muhammad and Barquq. In the middle of the road, where the street splits, is the wonderful recently restored **Sabil kuttub of Abd Arrahman Katkhudah,** with interior blue-and-white tiling. Taking the left fork, the small **Al Aqmar Mosque** on the right is reached down a few steps (the original street level over 1,000 years ago). We are now on the edge of a great regeneration area to restore the large Ottoman-period merchants' houses along Haret Ad Darb Al Asfar. Pride of place goes to the 16th-century **Bayt As Sehaimi** ⓭ (daily 9am–5pm; charge), which shows how the Cairo heat could be tempered with gardens, trees, fountains and cooling wooden window screens (*mashrabiya*). Music and theatre programmes are performed here.

Just before the Bab Al Futuh gateway is the **Al Hakim Mosque** ⓳ (daily 9am–5pm; charge), named after a Sultan generally agreed to have been completely mad. He hated daylight, dogs, women, honey and shop-owners, and was probably killed by his sister, whom he intended to marry. His mosque, with its distinctive minarets, was completed 1,000 years ago and has been restored by the Bohras, a sect of Islam strong in India.

Cities of the Dead

There are two vast cemeteries known as the Cities of the Dead, to the north and south of the Citadel. Opposite the Al Azhar Park entrance, across the other side of the Shari' Salah Salim expressway is the extensive area known as the **Northern (or Eastern) Cemetery** . Many 15th-century Mamluk Sultans are buried in large ornate tombs, protected by guardians who organised the funerary processions, anniversaries and festivals. Guardian families have always lived here, but as Cairo expanded, many others have taken up residence in other mausoleums. The City of the Dead is now a huge community with its own shops, schools and bus services.

The large domes and minarets of the three main tombs can all be seen from the expressway. The most northerly belongs to **Sultan Barquq**, completed in 1411 with double minarets. The open courtyard leads to a prayer hall beneath a chevron-patterned, mud-brick dome. You can see where the carved stone *minbar* was originally painted in blue, white and red.

About 100m/yds south along a dusty street is the slightly later **Bersbay Mausoleum.** The marble tomb is reached

Royal tombs at the Hoash Al Basha monument

through the prayer room, which has an exquisitely carved wooden *minbar* and ceiling.

Another 100m/yds further south is the 1474 **Mausoleum of Sultan Qayetbay**. Climb steps up to the prayer hall and then go through to the tomb with beautiful multicoloured windows. If possible, get access to the roof, where the real beauty of the decorative workmanship of the dome can be appreciated. Views from the top of the minaret are fabulous, and quite different from those inside the city.

Sections of the **Southern Cemetery** ㉑ are much older, some dating to the 12th century. Surrounded by walled areas of thousands of graves and tombs are two main mausoleums, both about 2.5km (1.5 miles) south of the Citadel. **Imam Ash Shafi'i** is a popular local saint, credited with founding one of the four main schools of Sunni Islam. He died in 820 and his **tomb** is the oldest part of the complex, dating

Ibn Tuloan Mosque

from 1211. Money and written wishes are piling up inside the tomb, which has a carved marble column marking the position of his head. It is poorly lit, but you can just make out large corner *muqarnas* (honeycombs) supporting the huge wooden dome. Pious Muslims make pilgrimage here, and there are sometimes anti-Western feelings. About 100m/yds

Gayer-Anderson Museum

away is the multi-domed **Hoash Al Basha**, containing the extravagant and colourful tombs of Muhammad Ali's family. The best views are from the roof, from where you can see the model boat placed on top of the dome of Imam Ash Shafi'i, representing spiritual enlightenment.

Ibn Tuloan Mosque

In 870, Ahmed Ibn Tuloan was the Abbasid governor who briefly seized control of the city and built a new centre north of Al Fustat. Within 35 years the Abbasids had regained authority and destroyed everything except the **Ibn Tuloan Mosque ㉒** (daily 8am–5pm; free), regarded as one of the finest and oldest mosques in the city, with many unique features. It is the only major mosque built from brick rather than stone, with the wall decoration and minaret inspired by the great Mesopotamian mosque at Samarra, where Ibn Tuloan grew up. Within the massive double walls, the atmosphere is always peaceful around the prayer hall, courtyard and fountain. Slide around on your shoe covers to see the green-and-gold mosaics with black inlaid text, decorating the *mihrab*, topped by a wooden arch. Restoration has been carried out sensitively after complete documentation of the site, including structural, material and soil analysis. Access to the minaret is at the rear of the inner wall, but take care, as the exterior spiral staircase has no handrails.

Still within the inner wall is the entrance to the **Gayer-Anderson Museum** ㉓ (daily 8am–4pm; charge). This is a wonderful museum preserved from the time when British Army Medical Officer Robert Gayer-Anderson lived here in the 1930s, with each room decorated in a different style. It is actually two connected 16th- and 17th-century houses, one of them with a *Sabil kuttub*, the *kuttub* appropriately turned into Gayer-Anderson's writing room. The guardian will point out access to the secret well. The roof terrace was added by Gayer-Anderson himself and embellished with Ottoman screens.

About 500m/yds to the northwest is another revered site of pilgrimage, particularly for women, the **Mosque of As Sayyidah Zainab** ㉔ (free; remove shoes). The tomb of the granddaughter of the prophet Muhammad is inside a shrine behind a solid silver grille, amid a forest of columns. This place is always lively, and the streets around the mosque are some of the most densely populated areas.

Coptic Christians

One of the names for ancient Memphis was Hikaptah, referring to the important Temple of God Ptah. This was corrupted by the Greeks into *Aigyptos*, from where we get both the words 'Egypt' and 'Copt'. Coptic Christianity belongs to the Oriental Orthodox Church which was brought to Egypt in the 1st century AD by St Mark, where it flourished throughout the next few centuries. The world's first monasteries were established in Egypt, often as remote settlements deep in the desert. The head of the Coptic Church is the Pope of Alexandria. Today the Copts make up about 10 percent of the population of Egypt.

SOUTHERN (COPTIC) CAIRO

St Barbara, 15th century,
Coptic Museum

The area known as Old Cairo generally refers to the Coptic site within the old fortified town that was established by the Romans at a strategic point on the Nile between Memphis and ancient Heliopolis. This Roman river port was called the 'River House of On' and known locally as Babylon. Following the spread of Christianity in Egypt, numerous churches were built here because of its associations with the Holy Family, who had visited on their way south to Asyut (see page 59). In AD641, Caliph Umar's conquering Muslim army laid siege to the fortified town before settling in a new area just to the north called Al Fustat, probably meaning 'city of tents'. Although Al Fustat became the seat of a military garrison for Arab troops, Babylon was preserved intact within its boundaries. The site is immediately outside the Mar Girgis metro station on the line towards Helwan.

Coptic Museum and Churches

One of the two massive Roman protective towers dating from Trajan's reign (around AD100), which once stood along the riverbank, is collapsed, while the other is now the circular Greek Church of St George. The gates between them lead into the **Coptic Museum** ㉕ (daily 9am–5pm; charge; no cameras). In the museum's care are 1,600-year-old texts found in a cave at Nag Hammadi in Upper Egypt, important scriptures that were not included in the Bible, including the Testament of Solomon and the Book of James with its controversial interpretations of the life of Jesus. The ground floor of the new wing exhibits remarkably well-preserved tapestry hangings from the 4th century AD and items removed from the 6th-century Monastery of St Jeremiah, uncovered at Saqqarah. Upstairs are gospels in Arabic, incense censers and a remarkable Ottoman-period wooden litter inlaid with bone and mother-of-pearl, used to carry wealthy women pilgrims to Jerusalem. To the right is the old wing, generally displaying objects from the nearby churches of Old Cairo. From this pleasant courtyard, steps lead down to the Water Gate, underneath Al Muallaqah, the so-called Hanging or Suspended Church.

The Church of the Virgin, **Al Muallaqah** (Suspended Church; daily 7am–5pm; free) is perched on the two bastions that were originally the southern gates of the Roman fortress. It dates from after the Arab conquest and has certainly

Al Muallaqah, the Suspended Church

been rebuilt many times. Try to visit during a service (Fri and Sun 8–11am), when the incense can be smelled as soon as you emerge from the metro station. A large plasma screen shows the priest's rituals behind the iconostasis, decorated with gold images of the saints, as streams of silver light from the high windows pierce the incense smoke like beams of light from heaven. Despite its modern appearance, it has a very rustic and ancient feel.

Geniza Documents

One of the greatest Jewish treasures ever found, the Geniza Documents give us a wonderful insight into the everyday Jewish life of the 11th and 12th centuries. *Geniza* means a 'hiding place' for sacred Hebrew books which must not be thrown away. Some 140,000 fragments are presently being studied at Cambridge University Library.

Across the street to the north, the circular **Church of St George** is an important site of pilgrimage for Copts, who slowly pass through a small shrine, acknowledging a golden faceless image of Christ. Colourful stained-glass windows do little to brighten an otherwise gloomy and dark building. In a crypt below are chains said to have been used to torture St George; they can be tried on for size. Many of the small churches inside Old Cairo are similar in style and often poorly lit.

An underpass leads to a narrow lane, and the nunnery of St George has another set of chains and a wonderfully kitsch mechanical St George thrusting his lance into the dragon time and time again, as he rocks back and forth. Around a couple of tight corners is the **Church of St Sergius** (Abu Serga), an important place of pilgrimage due to a crypt that claims to have once sheltered the Holy Family. The crypt is now out of bounds due to rising water level, but the church itself is a good example of a Coptic church. Further along the narrow lane, also below ground level, is the gloomy **St Barbara Church**, where shoes must be removed to enter the rear chapel.

Amid understandably high security is the modern **Ben Ezra Synagogue** (daily 8am–5pm; free), originally the site of a church, but then named after the 12th-century Rabbi of Jerusalem Abraham Ben Ezra. It claims much older associations, including being where the pharaoh's daughter found the infant Moses amongst the bulrushes, an entirely feasible claim considering that the Nile ran beside Old Cairo at that time. It was also the site of a great find in 1896 – the Geniza Documents. The synagogue once served the local Jewish community, but now stands in isolation, after people left the area during the wars with Israel.

Al Fustat

Just to the north of here is the large **Mosque of Amr Ibn Al 'Ass** ㉖ (daily 8am–5pm; free), built as one of Africa's first Islamic centres of worship and learning following the Arab

Pottery near Al Fustat

invasion in AD641, long before Al Azhar university was established. Today it is a very striking white building with a bright, open courtyard and high arched windows, set within its own pedestrianised zone. Carpeted throughout, the prayer hall is a forest of columns, some with old Arabic inscriptions, others said to have been miraculously whisked here from Mecca. This mosque became the focus for the new city of

The Nilometer from a floating restaurant

the Arabs called **Al Fustat**, built alongside the established Jewish and Coptic town of Babylon. This was a great centre for pottery and ceramic production during the Fatimid era, and there are still some modern potteries continuing the tradition. The ruined area of Al Fustat is to the east of walled Old Cairo, but with most of the site full of rubbish there is little to see today.

Also connected with this Christian area of Cairo is the **Abu As Seafain Monastery**, between Amr Ibn Al 'Ass Mosque and the Nile. North of here, on the eastern bank of the Nile, are the remains of a large hexagonal tower and **aqueduct** beside a busy traffic interchange. This tall structure was built in the 16th century to carry water from the Nile to the Citadel.

Al Roadah and the Nilometer

Walking west along any of the streets from Old Cairo will soon bring you to the narrow branch of the Nile, across which is Al Roadah island (*roadah* meaning 'garden' in Arabic). This quiet residential island is 3km (1.8 miles) in length and accessed

Umm Kulthum

In the Manisterli Palace complex is a museum dedicated to the life of Umm Kulthum. With the glut of popular singing stars today, it is difficult to realise just how important a figure she was half a century ago, when the music and poetry of her singing voice could reduce men to tears. Her life story from the poor rural Delta to international diva is well documented. Photographs of her with famous leaders show how popular she became, at a time when every Arab country looked to Egypt for inspiration.

by four vehicle bridges plus a beautiful ironwork pedestrian bridge at the southern tip, where there are three different but fascinating sights.

The prominent conical dome covers the **Nilometer** ❷. Dating from the Abbasid period, it is said to be the second-oldest Islamic structure after the nearby Amr Ibn Al 'ass Mosque. Nilometers were devices for measuring the level of the Nile, and this one was built on a site occupied by an earlier specimen. The guardian is keen to show the intricate decoration of the vertical shaft that reaches down to the river, accessed by steps. Before the dams at Aswan were constructed, the water rose every summer and the strength of the inundation was shown by the level of water covering the niches cut into the central vertical column. The greater the depth of water, the more the farmers had to pay in tax. From the bottom there is a wonderful view upwards to the ornate decorated dome, which is a later addition from the 19th century.

Sharing the tip of the island is the **Manisterli Palace**, built in the 1830s for the governor of Cairo, after whom it is named. It is a small Ottoman-era palace, which would not look out of place alongside the Bosphorus. As the newly adapted Centre for International Music, the main building is often shut, but it is possible to wander around the terraces for magnificent views across the Nile.

Towards the northern end of Ar Roadah is the **Manyal Palace**  (daily 9am–5pm; charge), hidden from the rest of Ar Roadah by a large wall. The buildings only date from the start of the 20th century, but it is a pleasant area of palaces and gardens, built by the son of Khedive Tewfiq. Beyond the entrance gateway are a series of splendid reception rooms and palaces in various Ottoman-era styles. The museum shows a fine collection of personal objects from the family of the Khedive.

Al Ma'adi

This south Cairo suburb is served by metro line 1, continuing beyond Old Cairo. After passing endless tenement blocks, the area around **Al Ma'adi** is a relatively wealthy residential area with strong Coptic connections. Settlements here go back further than pharaonic times, with evidence

Umm Kulthum

of early Neolithic human activity in small *wadis* east of the river, such as Wadi Digla and the Petrified Forest reserve. Al Ma'adi developed when the first railway line arrived over a century ago, and the ex-pat community now enjoys good shopping and sporting facilities, bars and beauty centres. A stroll alongside the Nile here is pleasant, and there are many riverside cafés and restaurants. This is one of the best stretches of river on which to take a felucca ride, with plenty of islands and no bridges.

Beyond Al Ma'adi the landscape opens out to views of heavy industry around Helwan, where the metro line ends.

Muqattam Hills

The escarpment rising to the east of Al Ma'adi is known as the **Muqattam Hills (Jabal Muqattam) ㉚**. Along its length are quarries where great slices of Tura limestone have been removed for thousands of years, including the blocks that were used to clad the Giza Pyramids so smoothly. Such a prominent vantage point has always been jealously guarded; the Citadel is built on a spur of the Muqattam Hills, and

Cleopatra's Needles

So great was the Roman obsession with exhibiting its control over ancient Egypt that there are more obelisks in Rome than in the whole of Egypt. However, not all the intended carved pillars made it to Rome. After defeating Cleopatra, Octavian (later Augustus Caesar) ordered the removal of the two granite obelisks outside the entrance of the Temple of the Sun at Heliopolis, but they only travelled as far as Alexandria. There they rested until the late 19th century, when Egypt presented one to London and another to New York. The ship carrying the obelisk to London almost sank and six men lost their lives; it was eventually raised beside the Thames in 1879.

even today there are military bases looking across Cairo. The development of **Madinat Al Muqattam** as a crowded suburb on the plateau itself has caused traffic to increase so much that an extra road has been blasted out of the rocks. There is little to see in the town itself, but there are some magnificent viewpoints over the city. Ask for the 'corniche' (korneash), which is a small roadway running along the western edge, with several makeshift teahouses and car parks offering spectacular sunset views.

The Baron's Palace

NORTHERN CAIRO

Heliopolis

The oldest centre on the east bank of the Nile was a city known as On, later called Heliopolis (City of the Sun) by the invading Greeks, who respected the established worship of sun god Atum. Ancient Heliopolis is where the Holy Family is supposed to have taken shelter during their exile, fleeing the wrath of King Herod. (According to Coptic tradition, they travelled to what is now Old Cairo, see page 51, and then further south to Asyut, where they stayed for several years.) The regeneration of the area for the influx of Europeans took place at the beginning of the 20th century, when Baron Empain, a Belgian industrialist, developed and modernised Heliopolis.

Muhammad Ali Pasha Palace

The Holy Family are said to have rested under what is known as the **Virgin's Tree** ❸❶ (daily 10am–4pm; charge) near Al Matariya. The original sycamore tree is long dead, but a third generation tree is surviving quite well on the site. Nearby is where the infant Jesus caused a spring of water to gush from the ground and there is an interesting little museum showing photos of locations relating to the sojourn of the Holy Family in Egypt. Paintings and biblical references of this journey are also to be seen inside the nearby **Church of the Holy Family**. Both sites are about 800m/yds northwest of Al Matariya metro station on the way to Al Marg. From the Church of the Holy Family, continue up the busy road for about 1km (0.6 miles), to the only remains of ancient Heliopolis, the 1940BC **obelisk** of Senusret I (daily 10am–4pm; charge), in a small park but surrounded by rubbish.

The main road from the airport offers arriving visitors a brief glimpse of some sights of interest as they speed past. The **Baron's Palace** ❸❷ is the strange Hindu-style temple set back on the left-hand side, built in 1906 for Baron Empain, the developer of modern Heliopolis, to be his own palatial residence, but now a crumbling ruin. On the same side of the road, but closer to the city centre, is the circular home of the **October War Panorama** (Wed–Mon; charge), surrounded by fighter jets, missiles and tanks. Inside are sculptures showing famous battles in Egyptian history, ending with a 20-minute narration in Arabic (English on headphones) of the 1973 October War against Israel. Actual film footage is shown downstairs. The tomb of the man behind that surprise attack on Israel is located about 2km (1.25 miles) east of here along the busy An Nassr highway, the main road to Suez. The **tomb of President Anwar Sadat** is below an open pyramid-style memorial, across the road from the scene of his assassination.

On the banks of the Nile is the **Muhammad Ali Pasha Palace** ㉝ (daily 9am–5pm; charge) in northern Shubra, sometimes referred to as the Shubra Kiosk or Shubra Palace, restored and reopened in 2008. Built as a pleasure pavilion in 1821 by French and Italian architects, it features a large central pool where the pasha would entertain his wife and 125 concubines and was once connected to the Abdin Palace by a grand boulevard. Water from four lion fountains pours over carvings of fish, creating a wonderful illusion of them swimming.

The pyramids at Giza

Surrounded by open colonnades, the rooms, including the beautiful Diamond Room, are built in various opulent Arab and Turkish styles. The palace is just to the west of Koleyet Al Zeraah station, the penultimate stop on the metro line to Shubra Al Kheima.

GIZA

The **Giza Pyramids** ❸❹ (daily 8am–sunset; charge) stand aloof from modern Cairo, set upon a plateau some 100m/yds above the Nile Valley and the nearby Mena House Hotel. But try to imagine the pyramids in splendid isolation, overlooking the green fields of the Nile, which was the case until only 150 years ago.

Pyramids

The builders of the Pyramids were kings of the 3rd–6th dynasties, covering the period 2686–2181BC. About 80 structures have so far been identified, but most are in a poor state of preservation, looking more like piles of rubble. Their use is still debated, but most experts agree that they were principally used as tombs for pharaohs. The evolution of burial sites from early *mastaba* (meaning 'bench' in Arabic) to step pyramid and then the true pyramids is a fascinating journey of spiritual ideals and 'hit and miss' engineering. One theory for the pyramid shape is that it represents the *Benben*, a triangular-shaped stone found in early temples, associated with the sun god Ra and the creation of life. In hieroglyphics, the *Benben* is represented as a pyramid shape.

Towards the end of his in-depth 1947 book *The Pyramids of Egypt* I.E.S. Edwards says that 'the temptation to regard the true pyramid as a material representation of the sun's rays and consequently as a means whereby the dead king could ascend to heaven seems irresistible.'

The Sphinx in front of the Great Pyramid

The Giza Pyramids are one of the most iconic images in the world, but even with all the facts and figures, it is still hard to believe that these ancient structures remain in such a good state of preservation. The sheer vision and workmanship of people 4,500 years ago, creating structures that would be the world's tallest until the 14th century is beyond belief.

King Khufu (Cheops in Greek), the second ruler of the 4th dynasty, took pyramid-building to this completely new level. Using the experience of his father, King Snofru, who built the first 'true' pyramid at Dahshur, Khufu thought of a burial tomb on such a gigantic scale that it would preserve him for eternity. His **Great Pyramid ⒶＡ** is built from an estimated 2.3 million blocks, weighing on average 2.5 tonnes each, fitting together so precisely that it is impossible to slide a sheet of paper between them. The angle of slope at 51° reached a height of 146m (479ft). The four sides are just slightly off the cardinal points, at a time when the magnetic compass was unknown.

Excavations at the **'Lost City of the Pyramids'** show that the stones were quarried from just below the pyramids themselves, about 400m/yds south of the Sphinx. This quarry was then filled with the debris from the demolished mud construction ramps. Study of the workmen's camp has revealed workers' houses, bakeries and tombs of the pyramid-builders, complete with inscriptions. Analysis shows that the workforce was more like 20,000 skilled builders taking 20 years, rather than Herodotus' account of 100,000 slaves over 30 years.

Entry to the internal passageways of the Great Pyramid is restricted to just a few hundred people each day. Tickets can only be bought on the day at 8am from the ticket office, so plan ahead. The forced tunnel, hacked out by treasure-seekers, leads first to the 'Ascending Corridor' and then the remarkable 'Grand Gallery'. The main burial chamber is a small room built of red Aswan granite, as is the large open sarcophagus still inside. Shafts leading upwards from here point towards heavenly bodies. Anyone suffering from claustrophobia or breathing problems should not enter.

The next pyramid belongs to his son **Khafra** (Chephren) **B**, and, even though it looks taller, it is actually smaller. This is because it lies at a higher elevation, on a platform cut out of the sloping hillside, as well as being built at a slightly steeper angle. Look towards the top, where a lot of the outer limestone casing is still to be seen. The internal structure of passages is much simpler, leading to a single chamber.

The third, smaller pyramid, at an original height of 66m (216ft), belongs to Khafra's son **Menkaura** (Mycerinus) **C**, with a single chamber located below ground. Its base area is less than a quarter of the other two, and nobody is certain why it is so much smaller. One explanation could be that his rule was cut short, but it is equally strange that none of his immediate successors have large pyramids.

Around the entire area are smaller ruined pyramids, *mastabas (tombs)* and pits belonging to members of the pharaoh's family and high officials, all following the king into eternity.

Each of the three main pyramids had a causeway sloping down to a canal connected to the Nile, at the foot of which was a funerary temple used for preparing the body of the dead king. During the construction of Khafra's funerary (or Valley) temple, a natural block of stone was uncovered that could easily be turned into a **Sphinx** , the mythical figure of a human head on a

The Sphinx

lion's body. The head of the Sphinx is made from the same hard rock on which the Pyramids rest, but the body is made from softer limestone that has eroded badly over the centuries. Several attempts have been made at repairing the outstretched legs and body, but the new constructions are not harmonious with the remaining sections. The carved face of the Sphinx is thought to represent Khafra himself.

It seems as though great pyramid-building, with its huge use of manpower and commitment, blossomed at this early period of Egyptian history, and could never be achieved again, not even to this day. There are some smaller pyramids from later periods, but these are considered poor imitations.

Between the two largest pyramids, on the southern side of the Great Pyramid, is the **Solar Boat Museum** **E**, a large glass building containing one of the **solar boats** (daily 9am–5pm in summer, 9am–4pm in winter; charge). It was found in 1954, dismantled in 1,224 pieces of polished cedar inside a narrow pit that can be seen underneath. An interesting series of excavation photographs and explanations of the 13 years of reconstruction is on the ground floor, together with original grass ropes and reed matting from inside the double-roofed cabin. The huge rebuilt solar boat rises above, with several walkways and platforms allowing good views of the remarkable workmanship. A slightly smaller boat, also dismantled in antiquity, was discovered in another nearby pit, but this has been kept *in situ* and sealed up again for preservation. The real use of these boats is unknown, but they might have been used for a single journey on the Nile

The solar boat, thought to have carried the pharaoh's body

to carry the pharaoh's body (there is a faint watermark), or for symbolic use in the afterlife.

About 1km (0.6 miles) beyond the Menkaura Pyramid is a **viewpoint** on the edge of the desert. Tour groups are driven there to take photographs across the sand, and to get hassled by souvenir-sellers and camel-ride touts. Take a look around this viewpoint, as there are some fossils in the sandy depressions showing that this was once under water. As you would imagine, security for visitors is tight, which is sometimes difficult given the scale of the Giza Pyramids area. Tourist police with machine-guns perched on camels is now a photo that many tourists take back with them.

A sunset or evening visit to the Pyramids is particularly magical. The daily *son et lumière* (sound and light show) is popular, with shows in several languages each evening.

Pharaonic Village

On the way back into Cairo, south of the point where the Pyramids Road meets the Nile, is the **Pharaonic Village** (summer daily 9am–9pm, winter daily 9am–6pm; charge). This island compound is the culmination of a lifetime's work by Dr Hassan Ragab, who studied the art of papyrus-making and the lives of the ancient Egyptians. Popular with children, it is a theme park-cum-education centre, with recreated temples, quarries, boatyards and scenes of everyday life along the riverbank. Actors play the parts of ancient Nile folk, in what is a crash course of Egyptian history, taking about half a day. The location is at 3 Shari' Al Bahr Al Aazam. Dr Ragab's **Papyrus Institute and Museum** is also located here, having moved from the houseboat just south of the Cairo Sheraton.

North of here are the extensive grounds of the **Zoological Gardens** (daily 9am–4pm; small charge). Depending on your point of view, this could be an interesting or depressing way to spend some time. The animals are generally well looked after, but come in for some abuse from the public. Whatever your thoughts of animal welfare, the grounds and walkways provide a pleasant location for a quiet stroll.

The zoo's main entrance at Meadan Al Gama'a is overlooked by the massive statue by Mahmoud Mokhtar (see page 34) entitled *Egypt's Awakening*. The wide road behind this leads to the centre of **Cairo University**. Just across the road are the **Orman Botanical Gardens** (daily 9am–4pm; small charge), home to specimens from around the world.

Running north from Meadan Al Gama'a in the suburb of **Ad Duqqi** is Shari' Ag Gizzah, along which is the **Muhammad Mahmoud Khalil Museum ㉟** (daily 9am–6pm; charge). The man in question was the Minister of Agriculture in the 1937 government, and admired everything French – especially art, but also culture, cuisine, architecture and women (his wife was French). This building, at 1 Shari' Kafour, was their original mansion, later appropriated by President Sadat. Today it houses a fabulous private collection of paintings that would not look out of place in the great national museums of Europe: eight by Delacroix, six by Millet, five each by Renoir, Sisley and Monet, with a few by Degas, Toulouse-Lautrec, Gauguin and Pissarro thrown in. The largest painting is a Nile scene by Eugène Fromentin. There are also Rodin sculptures, Limoges porcelain, ceramics, bronzes, tapestries and stained-glass windows.

OTHER ANCIENT SITES

Memphis and Saqqarah

The oldest centre on the west bank is at **Memphis ㊱** (daily 8am–5pm; charge), built at a point that could control both Upper Egypt (the Nile Valley) and Lower Egypt (the Delta). It was founded around 3100BC by the possibly mythical King Menes, said to have been the first to unite both Upper and

Lower Egypt, and so becoming the first king of the 1st dynasty. The god Ptah was later worshipped here at a great temple adorned by huge statues, but sadly there is little to see today, most of the constructions being of mud brick, which after centuries of neglect simply disappear back into the earth. Any heavy stone buildings have slowly sunk into the soft Nile silt, and remaining blocks have since been used elsewhere. Tour groups spend most of their time at the small building protecting the colossal statue of Rameses II, fallen in antiquity from the Ptah Temple entrance. The legs of the statue have been eroded, but the upper body, head and arms are beautifully carved and adorned with the king's cartouche. The workmanship can really be appreciated at close quarters. Statues and columns removed from the surrounding area of temples have been brought into the compound, including a remarkably well-preserved alabaster Sphinx.

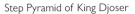

Step Pyramid of King Djoser

Later kings chose to rule further south from Thebes, but Memphis remained an important city for many centuries. The name Memphis is a later Greek variation of *Menfe*, a 6th-dynasty pyramid in the nearby necropolis of Saqqarah.

The site of **Saqqarah** ➐ (daily 8am–4pm; charge) lies about 3km (1.8 miles) west of Memphis, and is possibly named after Sokar, god of the burial sites. The famous Step Pyramid of Djoser can be seen appearing over the tops of the many palm-tree groves. A welcome addition to the site is the modern **Imhotep Museum** (entry included in site fee; no flash photography), opened in 2006 in an attempt to redistribute many of the Egyptian Museum treasures to more relevant locations. The many highlights include objects found inside the Pyramids and tombs, such as a delightful model wooden rowing boat with human figures from the tomb

Imhotep

Kings of the 1st and 2nd dynasties were buried in *mastabas*, small rectangular mounds of mud brick (which had strength limitations for high buildings). The exact role of Imhotep is unknown, but he seems to have been a high priest and official of King Djoser, and is seen as the first engineer, architect and physician in history. For the tomb of his king, Imhotep initially built a *mastaba* in local stone blocks, which needed precise cutting and handling. Having completed it, he found there was enough strength to build another on top, and so on. The achievements of Imhotep were recognised by later dynasties, which elevated him into a god, and also associated him with astronomy. The later Greeks identified him with their own god of medicine, Asklepios. Imhotep's undiscovered tomb is presumed to be somewhere near Saqqarah and may contain many of his secrets. To fans of modern cinema, Imhotep is better known as the inspiration for the series of films entitled *The Mummy*, showing him coming back to life and wreaking havoc.

of Khennu, a royal scribe of
the Middle Kingdom. The
mummy of King Merenra
I, who ruled for five years
from 2297BC, is the old-
est complete mummy yet
found. Also take note of
the haunting limestone bas-
relief of the 'Starving Men
of Unas' from the causeway
ramp of 5th-dynasty King
Unas, showing the ribcages
of the starving Bedouin,

Statue in the Imhotep Museum

before they are given food by the king. Allow plenty of time
for the visit, which helps to explain the importance of the
Saqqarah site.

Above the museum, on the edge of the desert proper, is the
funerary complex of pyramids, tombs and *mastabas* dominated by the **Step Pyramid of King Djoser**, the first king
of the 3rd dynasty. Entry is through the rebuilt Hypostyle
Hall, the narrow passageway of which is always a bottleneck
of tourists stumbling on the uneven floor. Once you are in the
open, the full magnificence of the world's first stone building can be appreciated. The architect Imhotep (after whom
the museum is named) first built a stone *mastaba* in which
to bury his king, but for whatever reason he then enlarged
it, building smaller *mastabas*, one on top of the other in six
unequal stages. Looking at the pyramid, you can clearly see the
separate structures inside. It is possible that the surrounding
life-after-death structures are copies of real buildings used by
the king in Memphis. One curious small annexe at the rear of
the step pyramid, known as the *serdab*, contains a statue of the
king (not original) able to look out at the world through two
eyeholes cut in the wall.

Mastaba of Ti, a high court official, at Saqqarah

This is also the area of the ruined early monastery of St Jeremiah, whose finds are now on show at the Coptic Museum in Old Cairo. There are some nobles' tombs beside the causeway leading to the small Unas Pyramid, located close to the Hypostyle Hall entrance. The extra ticket for these can be purchased from the booth beside the car park, but better versions are to be seen at the **northeast tombs** about 1km (0.6 miles) away, already included in the entrance fee. Not all are open, but entry should be possible inside at least two of the Mereruka, Ankhma-hor, Ti and Kagemni

mastaba tombs, near the Teti and Userkef rubble pyramids. All of the tombs are at ground level, with splendidly realistic painted and carved scenes of everyday life. In the Nile are fish, crocodiles and hippo, whilst around them are baboons, dogs and cattle. There is dancing and music, meat being cut for the festivities, and a parade of family members behind the dead body – scenes that have provided scholars with an insight into daily life in ancient Egypt. Look closely at the small human touches in some of the carvings – a fragile butterfly on a plant, tiny frogs by the Nile or a hippo biting a crocodile. Some life-size figures seem to be caught mid-pace, walking out of the tomb walls.

Entry to the pyramids is via a 45° shaft and then along small passageways, bent double. Beneath a ceiling full of five-pointed stars, pyramid texts inscribed in the burial chamber ensured a happy afterlife for the deceased. One of the amazing finds nearby was the Serapeum Temple of Apis Bulls, a maze of underground tunnels with giant stone sarcophagi for the bodies of dead bulls, but it is now closed for safety reasons. The whole area is full of burial mounds, pyramids and tombs, but it still needs proper excavation, and there are bound to be some exciting finds in the near future. The two pyramids to be seen south across the desert in the distance are the Bent and Red Pyramids at Dahshur.

Around the Saqqarah and Memphis area you'll notice many carpet schools and papyrus factories, popular with the large tour groups visiting the area.

Maydum and Dahshur Pyramids

Viewing these other pyramids means so much more when they can be put into context with neighbouring ones. Throughout the pyramid-building period, there were five major developments. The first was Djoser's Step Pyramid at Saqqarah around 2780BC, which had six steps and a burial chamber below ground. Half a century later, this was copied by King Snofru, the first king of the 4th dynasty, who planned an eight-stepped pyramid covered in limestone blocks. The remains of this structure, with its burial chamber above ground, is known as the **Maydum Pyramid** (daily 8am–5pm; charge), 55km (34 miles) south of Saqqarah. Also referred to

Maydum Pyramid

Detail of the Bent Pyramid

as the 'collapsed pyramid' due to the removed outer casing, it now looks like a ruined tower surrounded by rubble. The site ticket includes entry inside the pyramid, as well as the nearby mud-brick *mastaba* **No.17**, which contained the oldest red-granite sarcophagus, with some mummy remains but no inscriptions. Be aware that the security forces are nervous in this former military area, with its easy access to trouble spots further south.

Dahshur

King Snofru did not just rely on his Maydum Pyramid, as he then built the **Bent Pyramid at Dahshur ㉚** further north. The reason for the alteration of the pyramid's slope halfway up, from an angle of 54 degrees to 43 degrees, is unknown but his engineers might have calculated that it would be too tall and liable to collapse, or it could have been finished in haste. For whatever reasons, Snofru embarked on a third and final one, known as the **Red Pyramid** (daily 8am–5pm; charge), which was the first 'true' pyramid. Built with much shallower angles, it is a graceful construction, containing a single burial chamber above ground.

In spite of all this, it is still not known where Snofru was eventually buried. The Bent pyramid is about 3km (1.8 miles) beyond the Red Pyramid across a rough desert track. King Snofru's son Khufu learned from his father's experiments and embarked on building the fifth version, which became the Great Pyramid at Giza.

EXCURSIONS

All of these excursions can be undertaken as day trips from Cairo, but Alexandria would certainly benefit from an overnight stay. Many agencies will provide a car, driver and/or guide for all of these, but they can be completed independently using public transport.

Al Fayyum Oasis and Lake Qarun

A good highway leads 75km (46 miles) southwest from the Giza Pyramids to the Al Fayyum Oasis, which can be reached in one hour. The reference to an oasis is somewhat misleading, as the region simply became waterlogged with the annual Nile flood, when water sometimes flowed into this depression about 44m (144ft) below sea level. The resulting silt deposits made it as fertile as anywhere along the Nile Valley or Delta.

Lake Qarun

Karanis Kom Awshim

An ancient canal called the Bahr Yusef was dug from the Nile to ensure a regular water supply, which became a large reservoir known to the Greeks and Romans as Lake Moeris, of which Lake Qarun is the remains.

Approaching from Cairo, the first place of interest is to the left of the main road at a point that overlooks the fertile oasis. At the ancient site known as **Karanis Kom Awshim** (daily 8am–4pm; charge) a cult of crocodile worship existed. Dating from the Ptolemaic period, it has extensive ruins of a temple dedicated to the crocodile-headed god Sobek, a temple to Serapis and a later Roman temple to Zeus Amun. Inside the ruined mud houses are old millstones and olive presses. Security is tight, with armed guards present.

Lake Qarun ㊲ (Birkat Qarun) is a popular weekend retreat for Cairenes, offering vast open spaces and water activities. There are several pleasant lakeside restaurants serving fresh grilled fish, and opportunities to take a local fishing boat onto the lake. The main town is now known as **Madinat Al Fayyum**, but was previously ancient Crocodilopolis, where the reptiles were revered. This modern town is now overpopulated, with little to offer visitors other than some creaking waterwheels and a quick look at the heavily eroded 12th-dynasty obelisk of Pharaoh Senusret I, on a traffic roundabout.

The railway also runs here, but the service is amazingly slow and erratic. The Maydum Pyramid lies to the east of the town, and it is possible to connect the two excursions into one long day, but only with your own transport.

Suez Canal

There are three suitable places to see the Suez Canal – Port Said (Boar Sa'id), Al Isma'ileyyah and Suez (Asswayss) itself, all possible day visits from Cairo. The best choice is the mid-way point of Al Isma'ileyyah, for several reasons. Port Said is furthest from Cairo, and ships leave in convoys at 1am and 7am daily to transit the canal. Suez is quite a large city, and the canal is some way from the centre, with the ships also leaving early in the day, at 6am.

Al Isma'ileyyah ❹ is only three hours away by bus or shared taxi, and is literally a breath of fresh air after Cairo. The eastern edge of this pleasant, clean city is Lake Timsah (not part of the canal), along which are pleasant beaches and the only large hotel, the Mercure Accor. From here the superstructures of the giant ships transiting the **Suez Canal** can be seen about 3km (1.8 miles) away to the east. To get a better view, take a taxi to the local car ferry that crosses the canal to Sinai. The ferry sneaks between the massive ships every 15 minutes, transferring vehicles and people to the other side, which contains a war memorial and gardens. There are few places in the world where you can watch giant tankers and container ships glide past at 15km/h (9mph) so close and so quietly. The ships take between 11 and 16 hours to get through the canal, so you are almost certain to see a line of them around midday at Al Isma'ileyyah.

Take a taxi to the small regional **museum** (open daily 9am–4pm; admission fee) established in 1932, which has a good selection of objects, mainly Greek and Roman finds, including a large 4th-century mosaic with mythological creatures. One of the most impressive items is a strange Hellenised face on a marble coffin in human shape from the Ptolemaic period, found in 1983. The city is full of pleasant parks, small waterways and old colonial buildings along tree-lined streets. Near to the centre is the former house of Ferdinand de Lessops, the builder of the Suez Canal, and, close by, a mosaic of the grand opening ceremony. In the central town square is the large new mosque of Abu Bakr Saddiq. The return journey to Cairo can be made by train, but this takes up to four and a half hours, with a detour through the Delta city of Zaqaziq.

Alexandria

The Mediterranean influence of Greece and Rome has given **Alexandria (Al Iskandariyyah) ❹❶** a completely different feel to Cairo. With its coastal location and maritime history,

Building the Suez Canal

Napoleon's plan to build the Suez Canal between the Red Sea and the Mediterranean was abandoned when his engineers wrongly estimated there to be a great difference in the two sea levels. Half a century later, construction was started in 1854 by the Belgian Ferdinand de Lessops. The opening, in 1869, was a major event which transformed Cairo, where new palaces and residencies were built to accommodate the visiting heads of state and royalty. The commissioned opera Aida was not ready in time, so *Rigoletto* was performed instead.

The modern canal is 192km (119 miles) long with no locks; today about 10 percent of the world's shipping use it. Despite recent improvements, there are still limitations on the very largest ships caused by the 70m (230ft) clearance below the Road Bridge at Al Qantarah and the 16m (52ft) draught. The last set of figures to be published (for fiscal year 2009/10) reported revenues of $4.5 billion. In September 2011 the *Al Ahram* newspaper reported that an Italian supply ship paid the largest ever fee of $2.28 million for a single journey through the canal.

The Suez Canal

it is more like Marseilles, Tunis and Piraeus all rolled into one. This is where Cairenes come to play, relax and fish, if only for the day.

Whilst the rest of Egypt persuaded invaders to adopt ancient Egyptian culture, here the Greeks and Romans built as they did elsewhere. The only surviving Roman theatre in Egypt is in downtown Alexandria, and it was also the location for another of the Wonders of the Ancient World – the Pharos Lighthouse. The city has long been Egypt's interface with Europe, soaking up outside influences, as can be seen by the many Greek patisseries and lively bars. These and the beaches sweeping along the seafront to the east make the city unique in Egypt; in spite of having a population of 6 million, it often has the feel and appearance of a small town.

This is a place that is easily enjoyed by soaking up its history and culture and sampling the cooling sea breeze, even in the hottest of summers.

Close to the centre on the seafront is the newest attraction, the striking sloping glass facade of the **Biblioteka 'Library of Alexandria'** (Sat–Thur 11am–7pm, Fri 3–7pm; charge; www. bibalex.org), supposedly looking like the sun rising out of the water. Opened in 2002, this vast modern library, also containing a concert hall, planetarium and science museum, was inspired by the ancient Alexandrian Library. It is even more stunning inside, and much larger than it appears.

Looking out across the eastern harbour, the prominent low white building is **Fort Qayetbay** (daily 9am–5pm; charge). It was built in the 15th century using stones from the ruined Pharos Lighthouse. This is a relatively quiet place of wandering couples and fishermen, but with great views back to the city.

Between the main railway station and downtown are the **Roman ruins** (daily 9am–5pm; charge) discovered in the

Fort Qayetbay

1950s. Extensive excavation is limited due to the encroaching modern buildings, but the protected 'Villa of the Birds' has some fine mosaics, and the only Roman theatre yet found in Egypt.

The **Alexandria National Museum** (daily 9am–4pm; closed Friday noon for prayer; charge; no cameras) is just to the east of the Roman ruins on Shari' Fouad in a con-

Egypt's only Roman theatre

verted Italian-style pasha's palace. It contains many top class objects from around the country, covering the main historical periods over three floors.

Also of interest is the solitary **Pompey's Pillar** (built for Diocletian in AD293), the underground catacombs of **Kom Ash Shuqafah** and the ornate **Mosque of Abu Al Abbas Al Mursi**.

To the east of the city is a series of beaches, backed by high-rise apartments across an amazingly busy and twisting 'corniche' (korneash) road. Access to these suburbs of Shatby, Stanley and Glim is by taxi or the charming rattling trams that run a few blocks inland, departing from Ramleh tram station at Meadan Sa'd Zaghlul. Around this open square is the famous Cecil Hotel and classic café/restaurants.

Alexandria only takes about three hours to reach by express train, bus or shared taxi, so a day visit is feasible. The road between Cairo and Alexandria is acknowledged as one of the most dangerous roads in the world, with many accidents every day. There are several morning train departures, but for security reasons not all services can be used by Western tourists – check at the Ramssis Railway Station or tourist police office inside.

WHAT TO DO

SHOPPING

Cairo has been selling souvenirs to visitors for thousands of years, and there is certainly no lack of buying opportunities. From the moment you step off a tourist coach until you close the bedroom door, everyone seems to be selling something. Around each tourist location are stalls and hawkers, most hotels have shops, and if you still cannot find what you want, then there is always the intensive Khan Al Khalili bazaar. Making the sale is not the only driving force. Even though Egyptians are expert salesmen, it is generally done with a great deal of charm and hospitality. Even if you do not plan on purchasing anything, the offer is always made to sit down and rest, have a tea or coffee and a friendly conversation, in whatever language you choose.

Souvenirs are available everywhere, and it is worth looking around to see what the going rate is for something similar. Haggling is always expected. Outdoor stalls, such as those at the Pyramids viewpoint and in the Khan al Khalili bazaar, offer cheap and cheerful mementoes and presents, like stuffed camels (some of which sing) and obelisk paperweights. Shops in the downtown area usually have slightly better-quality goods, like inlaid boxes or trays and marble carvings. For the highest-quality replica items, such as statues and funerary jewellery, try the shops at museums or larger hotels. If you really know your subject, there are still amazing bargains to be found by searching through piles of old jewellery, carvings and silver in the many antique shops.

The exotic Khan Al Khalili bazaar

Antiques and Art

Works of art or antiques over 100 years old are not allowed to be taken out of Egypt, but there are plenty of younger items that are worth looking for. Zamalik has a few antique and curio shops behind 26th of July Street (Shari' 26 Yulyu):

Loft Interior Design and Gallery, 12 Shari' Sayed Al Bakri, Zamalik, tel: 2736 6931, www.loftegypt.com. Mounaya Gallery, 16 Shari' Muhammad Anis, Zamalik, tel: 2736 4827 (opposite the Safir Hotel).

There are several galleries around Meadan Tal'at Harb: Townhouse Gallery, 10 Shari' Nabrawi (off Shari' Champollion) enter at Shari' Hussain Al Me'mar Pasha, tel: 2576 8086, www. thetownhousegallery.com. Exhibitions and workshops of local artists, photographers and community art projects. Atelier du Caire, 2 Shari' Karim Ad Dawla, tel: 2574 6730. Oum Al Dounia, 3 Shari' Tal'at Harb, 1st floor, tel: 2393 8273, email: oumeldouniacairo@yahoo.fr.

Gold and Silver

People regularly sift through piles of old jewellery looking for rare and interesting items. But there are many attractively worked pieces to be found everywhere. Generally items are sold by weight.

Bargaining

Even if it is not in your nature to haggle over prices, it is all part of the buying process in Cairo. As a rule, try to settle for about half the initial price, or get something else thrown in for free. Walking away often drops the price.

Atef Wassef Silver Shop, 54 Shari' Abdel Khalek Sarwat, tel: 2390 3954 (at the Al Azbakeyyah Gardens end). Vast collection of ancient Coptic, Bedouin and Upper Egyptian metalwork and jewellery items.

For top-class gold and gems go direct to the factory of Eleish Diamonds, 11 Bayt

Al Kady, As Saghah, tel: 2591 7307 (opposite the Qalawoan complex along the Qasabah beside Khan Al Khalili). They have four showrooms around Cairo.

Papyrus and Cartouches

The most distinctive items to buy in Egypt are a papyrus painting or a cartouche. The art of making papyrus was lost until Dr Hassan Ragab researched and grew papyrus along the banks of the Nile in Cairo during the 1960s. Today every souvenir-seller has reams of papyri of every possible size and tomb scene. For the casual visitor it

Sheesha water pipes for sale

is difficult to distinguish real papyrus from artificial materials, and machine-printed scenes rather than hand-painted, and you usually get what you pay for, but not always. A 'Papyrus Exhibition' shop near the Pyramids can explain the differences, and you can make a choice.

A cartouche is a bordered oblong shape containing hieroglyphic symbols of a pharaonic name, usually seen carved into temple walls and columns. Your own name can be represented by hieroglyphic text, and many of the local guides can write this for you on a piece of paper. Given a few hours, you could also get this made as a gold pendant to hang from a necklace, which is uniquely Egyptian. Having your name

Papyrus with hieroglyphics depicting Egyptian mythology

painted as a cartouche onto papyrus is a double Egyptian exclusive.

Carpets and Cotton

The quality of carpets is very variable, but the cheaper rugs and mats are usually good value, being produced locally. There are many carpet shops around the Giza Pyramids and south towards Saqqarah, where you can see them being made. The quality of Egyptian cotton is well known, so any local cotton item is often good quality and value, even if it is only a white T-shirt or grey scarf. The long male *galabiya* dress is sometimes favoured by Westerners as a nightshirt.

Spices and Perfume

One of the most popular sections of the Khan Al Khalili is the spice market, where packets of good-quality spices do a brisk trade. Cumin, coriander, pepper and *shatta* (ground chillies and hot peppers) are all good for the kitchen at a fraction of prices back home. The art of the perfumier is much less popular than it was 20 years ago, when every tourist was expected to return home with a gallon of Eau du Nil. Still good value if you know your smells.

Books and Prints

If your interest in ancient Egypt has been stimulated, then there are several good bookshops with new and old and some reprinted titles:

Lehnert & Landrock have been respected oriental publishers since 1904. They have a shop that is part of the Nile Hilton Hotel and is opposite the Egyptian Museum entrance (tel: 2575 8006) and another shop at 44 Shari' Sherif (tel: 2392 7606/2393 5324), just north of Shari' Adly.

Useful for maps and travel books in Zamalik is the Diwan Bookshop, 159 26th of July Street (Shari' 26 Yulyu), Zamalik (tel: 2690 8184/5; www.diwanegypt.com), who also have seven other outlets around the city.

For framed prints, watercolours and oils go to The Readers Corner, 33 Shari' Abdel Khalek Sarwat, tel: 2392 8801 (off Shari' Tal'at Harb).

Shops and Malls

Downtown, there are many glitzy clothes shops along Shari' Tal'at Harb, but shopping for modern clothes and electrical and digital items at chain retailers is mainly at the large shopping malls located in the new suburbs and satellite towns around Cairo.

Locally produced rug with pyramid design

Towards the airport is the large complex of shops, restaurants, offices and hotels between Heliopolis and Nasr City called City Stars, 2 Shari' Aly Rashed, Star Capital 2, Heliopolis, tel: 2480 0500, www.citystars.com.eg.

ENTERTAINMENT

Cairo has a vibrant nightlife to cater for almost every taste, from classical and opera to casinos and belly dancing. Check listings in the papers and magazines.

Sound and Light show. One of the most memorable evenings is to visit the Giza Pyramids to see the *son et lumière* (daily; charge), with two or three performances each night in different languages. The seating area is opposite the Sphinx, as the ancient history is told using phased lights to highlight each pyramid or feature in turn, with actors speaking the parts of pharaohs. The lights are much more impressive than the dialogue. The English version is generally at 8.30pm in summer and 6.30pm in winter each day except Thursday (9.30pm summer, 7.30pm winter) and Sunday (11.30pm summer, 9.30pm winter). These days and timings can alter, so please

Moulids

A *moulid* is the celebration of a holy person, rather like a saint's day. Nothing in Islam encourages this idea, so it is probably inherited from ancient Egyptian times. The focus for pilgrims and visitors is on the tomb of the person itself, which becomes a great centre of socialising and entertainment as much as religious observance. The biggest crowds turn up for the *layla kebir* (big night) – the final night of festivities, especially when the Sufi groups parade and dance in the streets, amid frenzied activity. In Cairo, the biggest and most raucous *moulid* is that of As Sayyidah Zainab.

check beforehand. The website www.egyptsandl.com is often not working.

Cinema. One of the main forms of entertainment for local Egyptians is the cinema, which has had great appeal around the Arab world for decades. Some of the best actors, such as Adel Imam and Omar Sharif, are to be seen in both new and old films, which are in Arabic. New American high-action blockbuster films do get released in English, with most having subtitles. There are many cinemas downtown where tickets are cheap and great value, with every performance packed. Listings are in the local papers.

Opera. Performances of dance, classical and Arabic music at the Opera House on Gazirah Island are quickly sold out, so the problem is getting a ticket. The season starts in October, and a programme of events can be found at reception or

The sound and light show using the Sphinx and the Great Pyramid at Giza

The twice-weekly dervish show at the Wekalat Al Ghuri

online. Smart clothing is expected, with men requiring jacket and tie. The Opera metro station is nearby. Ticketing Office tel: 2739 0114; information tel: 2739 0144/0132; www.cairoopera.org. Some events are held at other locations, such as the Al Gumhureyyah Theatre, near Muhammad Naguib metro station.

Live music. In addition to events at the Opera House, there is a wide variety of live music, ranging from mystical Sufi to heavy rock. Check the locations themselves, such as the Al Sawy Culture Wheel Centre in Zamalik, tel: 2736 8881, www.culturewheel.com. The Manisterli Palace at the southern end of Al Roadah Island has some classical music events, but not on a regular basis. The excellent Tannura Group performs twice weekly at the Wekalat Al Ghuri (Wed and Sat 8pm; free) and should be at the top of your 'things to do' list. Often referred to as 'whirling dervishes', they perform Sufi dancing to live music and singing.

Many of the modern coffee shops have posters and adverts for performances, and a free monthly guide called *The Croc* is also useful. There are always plenty of free live events throughout the month of Ramadan, when people stay up for much of the night.

Theatre. Live theatre has always been popular in Cairo, with many acclaimed film and TV actors taking to the stage. Farcical comedies and family dramas are the main themes, and even though they are in Arabic, a visit to one of these classical theatres is always memorable. Some of the best long-running shows are filmed on stage and then repeated many times on television. Cultural centres sometimes have visiting theatre companies that put on more serious plays.

Belly dancing. Some of the highest-paid performers for a night's work are famous belly dancers, who gyrate suggestively at private weddings or parties. Public performances are usually part of an evening show at a nightclub along the Pyramids Road, large hotel or floating restaurant on the Nile. Shows start late at night and go on into the early hours, and can be expensive with entry fee, pricey food and drink and tips to

Egyptian Cinema

A Yemeni farmer and a Moroccan housewife might know little about Egypt, but they could name many Egyptian actors and even quote some of their lines from famous films. Cairo has always been at the heart of the Arab film industry, often being the only supplier of Arabic feature films in the region. Old black-and-white epics are endlessly repeated on televisions around the Middle East, making the actors international stars way beyond the Nile. Cairo-born actor Adel Imam has been making films for five decades and still pulls in the crowds. His 2006 movie *The Yacoubian Building* set box-office records, whilst dealing with taboo subjects such as homosexuality.

the dancers. Recent fundamentalist activity means that you are just as likely to see a belly dancer from the exotic east of Romania or Ukraine.

Casinos. Many of the top-class hotels also have gambling casinos, which are essentially for non-Egyptians, as a passport is needed for entry. Blackjack and roulette are popular games, using chips bought with hard currency. Most are open throughout the night.

SPORTS

Participatory sports

Horse riding. One of the great thrills is to ride a horse across the desert close to the Giza Pyramids, and there are certainly plenty of horses available for short rides of an hour or less. Longer, more tranquil rides can visit some of the other pyramids to the south. Early morning or late afternoon is best for avoiding the heat. There are many stables and riding schools located between Giza and Saqqarah where this can be arranged, often signposted from the main roads. Arab horse-lovers should visit the Al Zahra Stud Farm at Heliopolis (tel: 2633 1733).

Water sports. The only sporting opportunity on the Nile is rowing, which is very popular with young Egyptian sportsmen and women, especially on the canal beside Zamalik. For details, try the Egyptian Rowing Club (tel: 2393 4350). Unless you are staying at one of the big hotels, using their swimming pools can be expensive, as daily fees keep rising. Regular scuba-diving excursions are organised to the Red Sea by most tour operators.

Felucca rides

An enjoyable way to spend an hour or two is to hire a felucca for a graceful glide along the river Nile. Late afternoon and sunset are popular times, especially with a picnic and drink.

Sports clubs. A number of large sports clubs are situated in the centre of Cairo, but most of these are for members only. If you can get inside as a guest they offer swimming, tennis, squash, etc. Contact: Cairo Sporting Club, near the Sofitel Hotel, Al Gazirah, tel: 2748 9415; The Al Gazirah Club, Al Gazirah, tel: 2735 6000; The Heliopolis Club, Heliopolis, tel: 2291 0065.

Health clubs and gyms. For general health and fitness, there are several centres with varying quality of equipment. Many Egyptians like to keep fit, and there are often women-only times throughout the week. Gold's Gym has taken over the old Dr Ragab Papyrus Institute Houseboat, between the Sheraton Hotel and the zoo. Ex-pat havens such as Heliopolis and Al Ma'adi have many club and gym options.

Golf. Overlooked by the Pyramids is the 18-hole course at the Mena House Hotel (tel: 3377 3222; www.oberoihotels.com). Nearer to Cairo Airport is the 72-hole course at the

Riding near the Giza pyramids of Khufu, Khafra and Menkaura

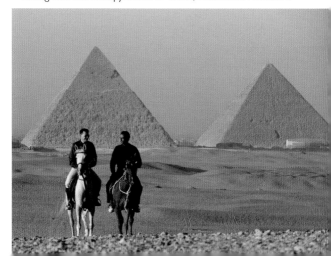

Katameya Heights Golf & Tennis Resort, New Cairo City (Fifth District), Ring Road, West Heliopolis, tel: 2758 0808.

Snooker, pool and billiards. Pool halls are springing up all over the place, usually frequented by local youths. Many pubs and bars in the larger hotels also have pool tables. There is a top-quality snooker room with four tables and bar on the 7th floor of the 'Galleria' annexe to the Ramses Hilton, tel: 2577 7444.

Spectator sports

Cairo is the home of the two biggest football teams in Egypt, Al Ahly and Zamalik, whose success or failure is passionately followed throughout the autumn and winter season. Al Ahly are record winners of both the league and cup. Ahly's great rival is Zamalik, and the matches between the two are great occasions.

Basketball and squash are also well supported, with Amr Shabana from Giza being one of the world's top squash players and former world champion.

CHILDREN'S CAIRO

With Cairo being such a large city, there are plenty of activities for children and the whole family. With safety in mind inside the city, Al Azhar Park is a great place to let children run around safely (summer daily 10am–midnight, winter daily 9am–10pm, tel: 2510 3868/ 7378).

Feluccas on the Nile

Dr Ragab's Pharaonic Village. An island full of activities for the whole day, including recreated ancient Egyptian buildings, landscapes and lifestyles.

The fun of the fair

Egyptian history is covered theme-park-style, from King Tut and Napoleon to Nasser and Sadat. An art centre offers hands-on pottery and papyrus-making, sculpting, painting and mosaics; 3 Shari' Al Bahr Al Aazam, tel: 3571 8675/6/7; www.pharaonicvillage.com, summer daily 9am–9pm, winter daily 9am–6pm.

Theme parks. Outside central Cairo, theme parks and large recreational resorts are continually being built. General amusements such as ice rinks, bowling alleys and rides are on offer at Dream Park (daily 10am–11pm; tel: 2855 3191) and Media Production City (also known as Magic Land; summer daily 10am–midnight, winter daily 10am–7pm, tel: 2855 5064/94) both in 6th of October City, near to the Giza Pyramids. In Heliopolis is Merry Land (tel: 2451 2316/7439). There are several water parks, such as Dreamland Aquapark (summer only daily 10am–10pm; tel: 2477 0099) on the main road to Al Isma'ileyyah, and Crazy Water (daily 10am–10pm summer only; tel: 2781 4564), heading towards 6th of October City. Water rides and the largest roller coaster in the Middle East are at Geroland (tel: 2477 1085/7; www.geroland.com), Al Obour City, north of Cairo on the Al Isma'ileyyah Road.

Giza Zoo. Depending on your views about animal welfare, this could either be an interesting or upsetting place to visit (daily 10am–5pm; tel: 3570 8895).

Railway Museum. While at the Rameses Railway Station, an interesting hour can be spent looking around this chaotic collection of Egyptian Railways memorabilia. The best part is clambering onto the Khedive's

Camel rides await at the Giza Pyramids

private train and seeing the insides of a steam locomotive, tel: 2576 3793 (see page 32).

Puppet theatre. Located near to Al Azbakeyyah Gardens, these performances are great fun for families, regardless of whether you can speak Arabic or not.

In Zamalik, there are often children's films shown at the Al Sawy Culture Wheel (see page 90).

Horse and camel rides. A visit to the Giza Pyramids can be beefed up with a gentle horse-ride, but with this being Egypt, the real way to cross the desert is on a camel. Take care when the beast gets up and down, and haggle loudly with the handler to get a more realistic fee.

Festivals and Events

January Cairo International Book Fair.
February International Tennis Championships.
March International Jazz Festival.
June Oriental Dance Festival with the emphasis on belly dancing.
August Cairo International Song Festival.
September/October Pharaohs Desert Car and Bike Rally, usually starting at the Giza Pyramids.
October Opera Aida Festival and beginning of the winter season.
November/December Cairo International Film Festival.
December Christmas concerts by the Cairo Symphony Orchestra.

Festivals fixed by Coptic calendar
7 January Coptic Christmas.
19 January Coptic Epiphany.
23 April Moulid of St George, celebrated at the Church of St George in Old Cairo.
1 June Moulid of the Holy Family at the Church of St Sergius.

Festivals fixed by Islamic calendar
Ashura celebration of the martyrdom of Imam Hussain on the 10th of the Islamic month of Muharram at Sayyedna Al Hussain.
Moulid An Nabi celebrates the birthday of the Prophet Muhammad.
Moulid of Al Hussain held on the last Wednesday of Islamic month Rabi Atani.
Moulid of Sayyidah Zainab great rowdy celebrations for two weeks in the Islamic month of Ragab around the Sayyidah Zainab Mosque.
Moulid of Imam Ash Shafi'I held during Shaban, the eighth month of the Islamic year, when a week-long festival consumes much of the Southern Cemetery.
Eid Al Fitr festival at the end of Islamic fasting month of Ramadan.
Eid Al Adha festival to mark Abraham's sacrifice.

EATING OUT

As the hub of the Middle East business and tourist trade, Cairo offers a wide variety of local and international cuisine to meet all needs. Cairo's location and historical influences produce menus that are a delicious combination of Lebanese, Greek, Italian, French, Turkish, Persian, Arabian, Indian and African flavours. From the most expensive meal in a top hotel to street food enjoyed by the locals, the ingredients are generally fresh and locally produced. Cairo's proximity to the Red Sea and Mediterranean assures a good supply of seafood and fish.

Top chefs are employed by the large hotels and enjoy a high reputation, with prices to match. Most restaurants in the city are locally run and are good places for Egyptian food at very reasonable prices. Most serve alcohol, but not all, especially small local places.

WHEN TO EAT

Cairo falls into the southern Mediterranean way of life when it comes to eating out. Breakfast can be taken at almost any time, with some cafés serving local dishes from 6am to midday. Lunch is generally quite late, anywhere from 2pm to 5pm, and often the precursor to a light nap. The evening meal might not begin until 10pm, and can stretch way beyond midnight. Hotels are mindful that many tourists prefer to eat earlier and serve food accordingly.

Karkadeh tea

WHAT TO EAT

Tasty food comes from a whole range of outlets. In the mornings, one of the best local breakfasts is a plate of steaming *fuul*, brown beans ladelled from giant silver cooking pots called *idras*. With a few discs of local gritty brown bread called *aysh baladi* and steaming hot cups of sweet tea, this is a great way to get the day moving. You are bound to see basket-loads of these breads being delivered from the bakery by bicycle around the city. Bread is the basic food source for most of the population and thus can be found in many shapes, but mainly as a type of pitta bread. Large hotels sometimes offer *fuul* in their vast breakfast menus, whereas smaller hotels are limited to more simple bread, cheese, omelettes, jam, tea and instant coffee, so it might be worth stepping outside for an occasional local breakfast.

Snacks

Throughout the day, there are delicious snacks to be bought around every corner. The popular *falafel* sandwich is a great standby for vegetarians, made from deep-fried patties of

Ramadan

The fasting month of Ramadan throws the whole process of mealtimes into disarray. The vast majority of Cairo's population do not eat, drink or smoke through the hours of daylight, but non-Muslims are permitted to use the restaurants and cafés that remain open. It is courteous not to eat, drink or smoke outside. The usual beer, wine and spirit shops close for the entire month, and many bars are also shut. During Ramadan, it is interesting to see, and even partake in, the vast open-air sunset street meals, known as *iftar*, which can become great social occasions. Eating, drinking and having fun carry on right through the night until the early morning meal, known as *suhuur*, the final meal before dawn.

Fuul flavour

Made from broad or fava beans, *fuul* is one of the most popular dishes in Egypt. There are several varieties: *Fuul Medammes* is seasoned with cumin, olive oil, lemon and spices. Other mixtures are with tomatoes, onions and peppers. *Fuul Mubarak* has a creamy sauce and eggs.

mashed *fuul* beans (*tamiya*) and parsley, placed into an envelope of local bread with finely chopped mixed salad, *tahina* sauce and sometimes pickles. In fact, pickled vegetables are a great local favourite, a selection of which is called *torshi*.

Giant vertical skewers of grilled lamb 'doner kebabs', known as *shawarma*, are now commonplace and make a filling fast food to be eaten on the move. Another popular snack is *fiteer*, a small, round pancake eaten plain for breakfast, with savoury toppings like a mini pizza, or with sugar and fruit as

Carving slices of grilled lamb to make a *shawarma* or doner kebab

a sweet. Some local eateries advertise their golden grilled chickens in rotisseries placed out on the pavements. A delicious sandwich is the cooked street food of *kibda*, small pieces of grilled liver placed inside a cut stick of bread, to which is added onions, chillies and spices (if you want it really spicy, ask for extra crushed chilli powder, called *shatta*).

Freshly made hummus

Lunch and Dinner

Menus for lunch and dinner tend to be similar, starting with a few plates of appetisers, which are quite substantial in themselves. *Tahina* is a thin paste made from ground sesame seeds with added olive oil and spices, whilst *babaganugh* is mashed aubergine with garlic, lemon juice and oil. *Hummus* is a dip made from chickpeas and now popular around the world. A dish imported from along the North African coast is *shakshouka*, a delicious blend of chopped lamb, tomatoes, onions, herbs and spices, topped with an egg. These starters are often accompanied by small dishes of pickled vegetables. With inspiration from abroad, salads have progressed greatly from the drab offerings of a few years ago. There are now wonderful Caesar, Greek, tuna and green salads, all prepared from high-quality local produce. A local style of thick soup is known as *molokiya*, which is like an oily spinach broth, sometimes with rice in it, and eaten with bread.

Another popular vegetarian dish is *kushari* (or *koshary*) made from rice, chickpeas, lentils, pasta, onions and tomato sauce. There are always plenty of main meals that are fairly standard, such as grilled meats and kebabs, chicken and pasta dishes, but there are some specialities. Pigeons (called *hammem*) are small delicacies, often stuffed with rice or grain, after being raised in pigeon houses that can be seen in rural areas, especially around Al Fayyum. Whilst there is little meat, what there is can be remarkably tasty. Pigeons and quails can also turn up inside another North African import – the *tagine*. Usually presented in an earthenware pot, a steaming *tagine* is a stew consisting of onions, potatoes and tomatoes on a bed of rice, with the choice of meat placed on top. Pasta has the generic name of *makaruna*, and usually comes as a slab of dense pasta cut from a large baking tray, to which is added a tomato- or meat-based sauce.

Care should be taken when eating street food, as some of the outlets might not be very hygienic and the food not very hot, which can cause stomach problems.

Desserts

Om Ali (meaning the 'mother of Ali') is a truly delicious and filling pudding, presented in a hot baking pot. It is made from milk, nuts, dried fruit, coconuts, cinnamon and cream, separated by layers of thin corn bread. *Baklava* is a light filo pastry stuffed with honey and nuts, whilst *kunafa* is similar but made with a more delicate shredded pastry. *Basboosa* is a semolina cake, dripping with syrup and lemon.

One of the great legacies of so much overseas involvement in Egypt is the large number of patisseries spread across the city, and many of the sweet, sticky pastries will be familiar from Greece, Turkey or Lebanon. Groppi is the most famous name of pastry shops, familiar to anyone visiting Cairo over the last 100 years. Established originally by a Swiss pastry cook and chocolatier, there are now two locations, at Meadan Tal'at Harb and Shari' Adly, the latter having a pleasant secluded garden. The alternative to all these rich, sweet pastries is a range of fresh fruit, depending on the season.

Drinks

Tea will be offered everywhere you go, invariably sweet, black and thick. Try to intervene beforehand if you would like it without sugar or with milk, but this is not always possible. There are many new coffee shops, as now found all around the world, serving a choice of beans and trendy styles, but in the traditional local coffee and tea shops, it will either be instant Nescafé or thick Arabic (Turkish).

Karkadeh is a really refreshing drink made from dried hibiscus blossoms, served hot or cold and originally from Nubia.

A delightful way to quench a raging thirst is with a local fruit juice from one of the many colourful stands. The choice depends on what is in season, ranging throughout the year with mango, orange, watermelon, strawberry, banana, pineapple and citrus fruits. Crushed sugar-cane stalks also provide a sweet, if somewhat gritty, juice. There is always the

Fruit juice stand

Coffee Shops

Every Cairo street has its local coffee shop, where *ahwa* (Arabic coffee) is speedily served to smoking domino players or avid newspaper readers. Fishawi's in the Khan Al Khalili and Wadi Nile coffee shop on Tahrir Square (Meadan At Tahrir) are great places to savour slices of Cairo life.

usual range of soft fizzy drinks as well.

Locally produced Stella beer comes as standard, export or premium lager flavours, whose quality has risen dramatically in the past few years. Recent additions to the choices of local beers are a weaker Sakara brand and two Meister beers, of which Meister Max is the stronger. Wines have also increased in quality to become fairly acceptable; the Omar Khayyam red is a safer bet than the Cru des Ptolomées white. Other additions are the Lebanese supervised 'Obelisk' red and white wines. Some top restaurants shun local beer and wine, only offering imports, but with a hefty price attached. Influenced by Greek *ouzo* and Lebanese *arak*, there are Egyptian versions with similar aniseed flavours, to be taken neat or with ice and water, whereupon the drink turns milky white. Locally produced whisky, vodka, gin and rum are for true connoisseurs only!

The communal smoking of a *sheesha* (or hubble-bubble) water pipe is something that you will see in many local restaurants and cafés. The tobacco itself is usually thick and pungent, and often mixed with other flavours such as apple or molasses. This activity is not confined to old men, and it is quite common to see a group of youngsters of both sexes sharing a *sheesha*.

TO HELP YOU ORDER...

apple	**toofa**	beans	**fuul**
aubergine	**berinjan**	beer	**beera**

bread	**aysh**	pasta	**makaruna**
butter	**zubda**	pepper	**filfil**
cheese	**jibna**	pineapple	**ananas**
chicken	**frakh**	potatoes	**batatas**
chickpeas	**hummus**	prawns	**gambari**
chocolate	**shokolata**	rice	**ruz**
coffee	**ahwa**	salad	**salata**
eggs	**beerd**	salt	**melh**
fish	**samak**	soup	**shorba**
liver	**kibda**	sugar	**sukkar**
meat	**lakhma**	tea	**shai**
meatballs	**kufta**	tomatoes	**tamatum**
milk	**laban, haleeb**	water	**moyya**
olives	**zaytoon**	watermelon	**bakhteerkh**
onions	**bassal**	wine	**nabeet**
oranges	**burtogaan**	the bill	**fattoura**

Serving mint tea in a cafe

PLACES TO EAT

We have used the following symbols to give an idea of the price of a three-course meal:

$$$$ over US$40   **$$$** US$25–40
$$ US$10–25   **$** under US$10

CAIRO

DOWNTOWN

Alfy Bey $ *3 Shari' Al Alfy, tel: 2577 1888/4999.* Grand old place serving good food since 1938. Efficient with a limited menu and good value, specialising in kofta, kebabs and stuffed pigeon. A loyal local clientele means there is a genuine Egyptian atmosphere. Tables spread out from the interior onto the street, but it's fairly quiet as it's within the pedestrianised section, at the Shari''Urabi end.

Estoril $$ *12 Shari' Tal'at Harb, tel: 2574 3102.* Interesting place down a dark alley behind the Air France office. It opened in 1959 and is said to be the oldest restaurant around Tahrir Square (Meadan At Tahrir). It is still extremely popular with ex-pats, and has a loyal clientele. Good vegetarian and Lebanese selections. Serves beer and wine.

Felfela $ *15 Shari' Hoda Shaarawi, tel: 2392 2833.* Lively and atmospheric hangout for budget travellers as well as those seeking a bit of local cooking in the heart of downtown, not far from Meadan Tal'at Harb. The authentic Egyptian menu consists of many hummus, falafel and other vegetarian dishes, as well as kebabs, pigeon stuffed with bulgur, and marinated quail; it also has one of the best Om Ali desserts around. This is the original restaurant, as can be seen from all the celebrity photos, but now has several outlets around the city.

Grazie $ *2nd floor, Ramses Hilton annex, tel: 2579 3636.* Good-value Italian food served quickly, and handy for the Egyptian

Museum. Next door there is a similar place called Al Hamra ($) offering Lebanese dishes.

La Chesa $$$ *21 Shari' Adly, tel: 2393 9360/5768.* Good-quality European food in a mellow atmosphere, with slightly upmarket prices.

Osmanly $$$–$$$$ *Kempinski Nile Hotel, 12 Shari' Ahmed Ragheb, Garden City, tel: 2798 0000, www.kempinski.com/cairo.* Atmospheric restaurant within a quality new hotel, not far from the British Embassy. Offers the best Turkish-style cuisine in the city, from tangy appetisers, through succulent meat main courses to delicious desserts, all within stylish Ottoman decor. Open daily noon–1am.

Taboula $$–$$$ *1 Shari' Latin America, Garden City, tel: 2792 5261, www.taboula-eg.com.* Find Middle Eastern cuisine with Lebanese origins at this comfortable and casual location, not far from the new Kempinski Hotel. Perfect for local businessmen and embassy staff at lunchtime, mellowing out in the evenings with subtle music and *sheesha* pipes. Great mezze, mains and desserts all washed down with Lebanese spirits, wines and beers.

Tamarai Bar and Restaurant $$$–$$$$ *Korneash An Nil, Nile City Towers, 2005c, Bulaq, tel: 2461 9910; www.tamarai-egypt.com.* This trendy new rooftop nightspot is the place to be seen, whether lounging on the large sofas or drifting around the expansive patios. It specialises more in nightlife than food, providing a modern setting for the Egyptian cocktail crowd.

FLOATING RESTAURANTS

Nile Peking $$$ *tel: 2531 6388.* This is moored at the southern end of Al Roadah Island near the Nilometer, not far from Old Cairo and the Mar Girgis metro station. From here it has a great stretch of Nile river to navigate without bridge restrictions. Part of the Peking Restaurants group, this operates twice nightly and some afternoons, offering set menus on river cruises, and a wider choice when moored during the daytime. Some theme nights.

Scarabee $$$$ *tel: 2274 3444.* One of several floating restaurants outside the Four Seasons Hotel, just north of Al Roadah. Great place for a sundowner on one of the open decks whilst it remains moored until it gets dark. Runs two cruises each night, one from 7.30pm, the other from 10pm, when it glides along the river with wonderful views along each bank. The floor show is the usual combination of belly dancing, local dancing and live music.

ZAMALIK

Abou Al Sid $$–$$$ *Off 26th of July Street (Shari' 26 Yulyu), Zamalik (near Maison Thomas), tel: 2735 9640, www.deyafa.net.* Atmospheric Egyptian bar-restaurant, successfully recreating an oriental colonial club feel with old furniture and decor. The local speciality is *molokiya*, a thick soup. Mixes modern and old local music, and offers *sheesha* smoking. Reservation required. Other franchises can be found further out at Al Muhandesseen, Al Ma'adi and at City Stars.

Dido's al-Dente $ *corner of Shari' Taha Hussein and Shari' Bhagat Ali , Zamalik (not far from President Hotel).* Not easy to find, but well worth it for the fabulous pasta dishes at bargain prices. Very small, often with long queues outside.

Four Corners $$ *4 Shari' Hasan Sabri, Zamalik, tel: 2736 2961/5640.* Four locations in one place, comprising French, Italian and Chinese restaurants and a British pub. All serve alcohol, with the Italian La Piazza the pick of the bunch.

L'Aubergine $$$$ *5 Shari' Al Sayed Al Bakri, Zamalik, tel: 2735 6761.* A popular gathering place for vegetarian ex-pats and young Egyptians before they move on to noisier places. The upstairs bar is popular and has an in-house DJ.

La Bodega $$ *157 26th of July Street (Shari' 26 Yulyu), Zamalik, tel: 2735 0543/6761.* On the first floor of a period building with a sophisticated Asian interior, this is more of a bistro and trendy hangout than a restaurant, but is great value, especially the set menus.

Sequoia $$–$$$ *end of Shari' Abu Al Feda, Zamalik; tel: 2735 0014; www.sequoiaonline.net.* Great location on the northern tip of Al Gazirah Island, overlooking the Nile on all sides. A wonderful place for relaxing and chilling with friends, either on the terrace or in the tent-like structure. This is where hip Cairo mixes with middle-class families and ex-pat foreigners in a very smooth atmosphere. Just lie back on one of the comfortable sofas, have a drink and smoke a *sheesha* with one of the 30 flavours of tobacco, or try out the excellent menu with plenty of Oriental dishes. Book ahead as this is hugely popular.

FLOATING RESTAURANTS

The Blue Nile $$$ *9a Shari' Saraya Al Gazirah, Zamalik, tel: 2735 3114, www.bluenileboat.com.eg.* Has several restaurants serving Moroccan, Lebanese (good *mezze*), Tex-Mex, and Asian (highly recommended for sushi) cuisine, as well as a piano bar and patisserie. Some open all day, others only during the evening, when dinner is accompanied by dance, live music and a DJ. Great views at night across the river, even though it stays moored.

Le Pacha 1901 $$$ *Shari' Saraya Al Gazirah, Zamalik, tel: 2735 6730, www.lepacha.com.* Award-winning eatery offering Far Eastern, Italian, French and Egyptian restaurants, all on board a former Pacha's private luxury boat from Upper Egypt. Also has bars and cafés for lighter fare. This is a floating restaurant that does not leave its mooring point.

EASTERN CAIRO

Al Azhar Park has four outdoor restaurants and cafés, each with glorious views across the Islamic part of the city. The higher restaurant is more formal and often needs to be reserved as it is extremely popular.

Fishawi's Traditional Café $ *located deep inside the Khan Al Khalili bazaar along a narrow alleyway.* Never any room and a real tight squeeze, especially in the evenings, but an atmospheric place to watch local sellers and traders pass amongst the crowds. Focus is on drinks rather than food.

Naguib Mahfouz Restaurant and Cafe $$$ *5 Sekket Al Badistan , Khan Al Khalili, tel: 2590 3788/2593 2262.* Located right in the heart of the bazaar area, and known by everyone. Formerly a small café frequented by Nobel award-winner Naguib Mahfouz, but now sent upmarket by the new owners Oberoi. Serves snacks and drinks rather than main courses. Ideal place for taking some time out from a hot wander around the crowded bazaar. Live Oriental music. Popular with visiting tour groups.

NORTHERN CAIRO

Esmak e'Douran $ *Shari' Shubra (just south of Rod Al Farag metro station).* This small seafood joint in crowded Shubra suburb attracts locals from all over the city for the quality of its fresh fish. The name means 'king of shrimps' and it certainly is.

GIZA

Andrea's $ *59–60 Marioutiya Canal, Giza, tel: 2383 1133.* Good Egyptian restaurant that is famous for its spit-roasted chicken served with tasty mezze and salads. In summer you can eat in the airy gardens, and there is a dining room for the chillier winter evenings. Lunchtime is often busy with tour groups, so for a more authentic atmosphere come in the evenings, although be sure to bring mosquito protection.

Christo $$$ *10 Pyramids Road (Shari' Al Ahram), Giza, tel: 3383 3582.* Wonderful selection of seafood accompanied by fabulous views of the pyramids from the terrace.

Fish Market $$$$ *26 Shari' An Nil, Giza, tel: 35709694.* One of several floating restaurants with the same name, others located at Al Ma'adi and downtown. So-called as the plentiful fresh fish and seafood is set out like a market for you to select your catch, pay by weight and let the cook do the rest. Good quality.

Pyramid's Tivoli $$$ *on Cairo-Alexandria Road, off Meadan al Remaya, Haram, tel: 3382 6555.* Café, lounge bar, restaurant and nightclub featuring an Egyptian show of *tannura* and belly dancing. One of many similar establishments, especially along the Pyramids Road, where the food comes second to the nightlife.

AL MA'ADI

Abou Al Sid $$ *45 Shari' #7, Al Ma'adi, tel: 2380 5050, www.deya-fa.net.* Another of the franchise outlets with good Egyptian food, and a great atmosphere. Perfect if you're looking for local dishes, a *sheesha* and beer with friends.

Fish Market $$$ *on the bank of the Nile, just south of the Sofitel Hotel, tel: 2380 4250.* One of the well-known chains, selling high-quality fresh fish in a beautiful location.

Fusion $$$ *on the bank of the Nile, just south of the Sofitel Hotel, tel: 2380 0210/0174.* Modern Far Eastern food, with a good-value set menu. Overlooks the Nile.

Max's Restaurant $$$ *17 Shari' # 263, New Al Ma'adi, tel: 2516 3242.* European menu with the Italian dishes recommended.

ALEXANDRIA

Athineos $$ *between Ramleh and the sea, tel: 03-482 0421.* More of a coffee snack bar rather than a restaurant, but atmospheric thanks to the mirrored interior, which sometimes turns into a nightclub.

Samakmak $$$$ *42 Kasr Ras At Tin, Al Bahry, tel: 03-481 1560.* As the name suggests – samak is Arabic for fish – this is a fish speciality restaurant, next door to the fish market. Great food, but out of the centre.

Trianon $$ *corner of Meadan Sa'd Zaghlul and Ramleh, tel: 03-482 0986.* Splendidly ornate throwback to colonial times in both the restaurant and café sections. Equally pleasant surroundings for breakfast, lunch or dinner.

A–Z TRAVEL TIPS

A Summary of Practical Information

A

ACCOMMODATION (see also Youth Hostels and list of Recommended Hotels)

Cairo offers a wide range of accommodation, from small independent hotels to the best international chains with facilities for business and leisure visitors. Staying in the downtown area can be noisy and chaotic, but a wealth of attractions can easily be reached by metro, taxi or on foot. Most hotels can be paid with credit cards, but some of the smaller places will only accept US dollars, euros or sterling cash.

hotel	**fondu**
how much?	**bi kam?**

AIRPORT

The new third terminal for international flights (airport code CAI) has doubled capacity. 'Meet and assist' is offered by many hotels; otherwise pay for an 'official' airport taxi or negotiate with eager drivers outside. The 15km (10-mile) transfer into central Cairo will take about 30 minutes at night, and upwards of an hour during the day.

When departing, surplus Egyptian pounds can be spent at the food stalls, restaurants and shops once through passport control. There is no departure tax to pay. Cairo International Airport, tel: 2267 5822, www.cairo-airport.com.

B

BOAT HIRE

A pleasant felucca boat ride on the Nile can be undertaken at any time of night or day, but sunset is the most popular, especially if you take a picnic. Hourly rates are negotiated by haggling. From outside the Nile or Ramses Hilton hotels, the boats can realistically only ply across the river and back because of the bridges, whereas from outside the Semiramis InterContinental, further south beyond Kubri At Tahrir, they have the scope to go as far as Al Roadah. Feluccas hired from Al Ma'adi can weave in and out of the small islands. Take insect repellent to avoid being bitten in the evening.

BUDGETING FOR YOUR TRIP

Unlike Luxor and Sharm El Sheikh, there are few charter flights direct to Cairo from Europe. Bring an International Student Identification Card (ISIC) for discounts on site entry fees, internal air and rail travel and some accommodation and restaurants.

The following prices in LE (Egyptian Pounds) and US$ will give a rough idea of how much you will spend.

Airport transfer. From Cairo international airport to Tahrir Square (Meadan At Tahrir), 60LE
Car Hire. From US$60 per day (*see Car Hire*)
Guides. Official guide for a two-hour tour of the Egyptian Museum or Pyramids, 100–150LE
Hotels. Probably your largest expense, costing US$20–500 per night (*see Recommended Hotels*)
Internet cafés. 5–20LE per hour
Meals and drinks. Breakfasts are normally included in room rates. A set menu or buffet lunch/dinner in a two-/three-star hotel or site restaurant will be 70–100LE; in a four-star hotel or floating restaurant, 150–200LE. For an evening meal in a city restaurant, budget 100–150LE. For a soft drink/coffee in a café, allow 5–10LE.
Sightseeing. Admission to museum/antiquities site, 10–60LE
Taxis. Trip across Cairo of 3km (2 miles), 30LE; from downtown to the pyramids, 50LE

C

CAR HIRE (see also Driving)

You would need a very good reason to hire a self-drive car and attempt to take on Cairo. The cost of hiring a car with a driver for a day, week or month would be much the same and a lot more flexible. Most tourist sites are accessible with public transport or taxis, and even a 4x4 adventure to the Western Desert and oases could be easily arranged through a local tour operator. If you insist on hiring a car, then make sure you have plenty of insurance for every eventuality.

You must have an International Driving Permit and be at least 25 years old. Local and international hire companies have desks at some of the major hotels. Avis (www.avisworld.com) has several offices around the city, including at the airport (tel: 2265 2429) and the Nile Hilton (tel: 2579 2400); Budget (www.budget.com) also has an office at the airport (tel: 2265 2395) and in Ad Duqqi (tel: 2762 0518).

CLIMATE

Think of Cairo as a city in the desert with only two main seasons – mild winters and hot summers. Temperatures throughout the year are between 12 and 25°C (53 and 77°F), but it can climb to over 40°C (104°F) in the summer months of June, July and August. The strong *khamseen* wind occasionally blows through the city from February to April, bringing unpleasant dust and sand from the Sahara, raising the humidity.

Rainstorms are unusual, but do occur in late winter.

CLOTHING

Loose-fitting clothes made from natural fibres are best in summer, when temperatures get uncomfortably hot. Shorts are not acceptable in the city for either sex, and women especially should make sure never to reveal too much flesh. Arms and legs should be covered for sun protection, local respect and when visiting religious sites.

Women wearing unsuitable clothing will be handed a cloak at sites such as the Muhammad Ali Mosque in the Citadel. Bring a sunhat, high-factor sun cream and sunglasses.

In winter a waterproof jacket is handy. Use layers of clothing to keep warm in the cold wind. Make sure to bring comfortable walking shoes or trainers, as many of the pyramid sights are on sandy, uneven terrain.

Some top-class restaurants have dress codes such as jacket and tie for men, and you will find that Cairenes dress up when going out.

CRIME AND SAFETY (see also Police)

The main concern is petty theft. The vast majority of Egyptians are friendly and helpful, but a few opportunists seek out tourists for pickpocketing or scams to catch you off-guard. Always keep low-value banknotes handy and never carry wallets or purses in back pockets or open them in public. Avoid having an expensive digital camera or bag slung over a shoulder where it can be easily grabbed. Take special care in the narrow alleys of the Khan Al Khalili bazaar, and at rush hour if using the metro, local buses or suburban trams. If anything is stolen, report it at a police station and obtain a report for insurance purposes. Always take care crossing roads.

Egypt has suffered some terrible terrorist attacks in the past decade, with bombings and shooting of tourists in the centre of Cairo. However, these were carried out by religious extremists and do not indicate a general dislike of tourists amongst the population. The authorities have set up security checks at all the main hotels and tourist sites.

D

DRIVING (see also Car Hire)

If you intend to drive a car you will need your national licence, international driving permit and photocopies of your passport and visa. Most visitors only drive if they are bringing in their own vehicle (or motorbike), as some off-road enthusiasts do from Europe. All private vehicles entering Egypt must have a *carnet de passage* from an automobile club in the country of registration or pay customs duty. Vehicles are initially imported through Alexandria, Port Said or Suez.

Road conditions. Most local drivers don't seem to obey any rules, so be alert at all times. Cars overtake in the face of oncoming traffic, and pull on and off the highway without indicating. Vehicles that in many countries would be deemed unfit for the road circulate freely in Egypt.

Rules of the road. In theory Egyptians drive on the right and overtake on the left, though in practice anything goes. Speed limits are 100kmh (62mph) on dual highways and 90kmh (56mph) on other roads, unless otherwise indicated.

Fuel. Fuel is inexpensive and sold by the litre.

Parking. Finding a place to park in Cairo is a challenge. Most large hotels have a garage, but clients may be charged for its use.

Breakdown and assistance. There are no breakdown services in Egypt, but in case of breakdown or accident you can call the Red Crescent, which operates a network of garages. Ask for their telephone number when you rent the vehicle. For more information on assistance, contact the Automobile Club of Egypt, 10 Shari' Qasr An Nil, Cairo, tel: 2574 3355.

E

ELECTRICITY

Egypt uses 220–240v/50Hz current, so most European appliances will be fine. Sockets mainly take standard Continental European round two-pin plugs. Electricity supply is generally good and reliable. US goods on 110v will need a transformer.

EMBASSIES AND CONSULATES

Australia: World Trade Centre 11th Floor, 1191 Korneash An Nil, Bulak, Cairo, tel: 2575 0444; www.egypt.embassy.gov.au.

Canada: 26 Shari' Kamel Al Shenawy, Garden City, Cairo, tel: 2791 8700, www.canadainternational.gc.ca/egypt-egypte/index.aspx?view=d.

Ireland: 22 Shari' Hassan Assem, Zamalik, Cairo, tel: 2735 8264; www.embassyofireland.org.eg/home/index.aspx?id=41539.

New Zealand: Level 8, North Tower, Nile City Towers, 2005c Korne-ash An Nil, Bulaq, Cairo, tel: 2461 6000, www.nzembassy.com/egypt.

South Africa: 11 Road 200/203, Degla, Al Ma'adi, Cairo, tel: 2521 3218; www.dfa.gov.za/foreign/sa_abroad/sae.htm.

United Kingdom: 7 Shari' Ahmed Ragheb, Garden City, Cairo, tel: 2791 6000, http://ukinegypt.fco.gov.uk/en/. The consular section can be contacted by telephone on 2791 6000, Sunday–Thursday 9am–2pm, and opens for personal callers 9.30am–1.30pm except holidays.

United States: 5 Shari' Latin America, Garden City, Cairo, tel: 2797 3300.

For information about visas and visits see www.touregypt.net/us consulates.htm.

In Australia (also for New Zealand): Egyptian Consulate, Level 6, 50 Market Street, Melbourne, VIC 3000, tel: 03-9614 0710. Consulate General of Egypt, Level 3, 241 Commonwealth Street, Surrey Hills, NSW 2010, tel: 02-9281 4844, www.egypt.org.au. Egyptian Embassy, 1 Darwin Avenue, Yarralumla, Canberra, ACT 2600, tel: 062-273 4437/8.

In Canada: Egyptian Consulate, 1 Place Ville Marie, #2617, Quebec, H3B 4S3, tel: 514-866 8455/6/7. Egyptian Embassy, 454 Laurier Avenue East, Ottawa, Ontario KIN 6R3, tel: 613-234 4931/35; email:egyptemb@sympatico.ca.

In Ireland: Egyptian Embassy, 12 Clyde Road, Dublin 4, tel: 01-606 566/718.

In South Africa: Egyptian Embassy, 270 Bourke Street, Pretoria, tel: 012-343 1590/1.

In the UK: Egyptian Consulate, 2 Lowndes Street, London SW1X 9ET, tel: 020 7235 9719; http://egypt.embassyhomepage.com. Egyptian Embassy, 26 South Street, London, W1K 1DW, tel: 020-7499 3304.

In the US: Egyptian Consulates: 1110 Second Avenue, New York, NY 10022, tel: 212-759 7120/1/2; 3001 Pacific Avenue, San Francisco, CA 94115, tel: 415-346 9700; 1990 Post Oak Boulevard, Suite 2180, Houston, TX 77056, tel: 713-961 4915; 500 N. Michigan Avenue, Suite 1900, Chicago, IL 60611, tel: 312-828 9162. Egyptian Embassy, 3521 International Court NW, Washington, DC 20008, tel: 202-895 5400; http://www.egyptembassy.net/.

EMERGENCIES

Report any emergency to the nearest police or army personnel. Emergency telephone numbers are:

Police: **122**
Tourist Police: **126** (also Cairo 2390 6028)
Ambulance: **123** (also Cairo 2574 3237)
Fire: **180** (also Cairo 2391 9364)

| Help me! | Il ha ooni! |
| Call a doctor | ayzin doktor |

G

GAY AND LESBIAN TRAVELLERS

Homosexuality is technically illegal in Egypt, but some couples do have same-sex relationships, and certain nightclubs and bars are gay hang-outs. Gay and lesbian visitors will encounter few problems as long as they are discreet and cautious about any outward signs of affection towards each other. Local men often greet one another with kisses and hold hands, but this is not the sign of a gay relationship.

GETTING THERE

By air. Cairo is served by many international airlines. Most major European airlines fly direct to Cairo, including British Airways, BMI,

Lufthansa, Air France, KLM, Alitalia, Iberia, Austrian Airlines, and Swiss. All have offices in Cairo (British Airways is at Meadan At Tahrir; tel: 2578 0743/4/5; www.ba.com).

Egypt Air (9 Shari' Tal'at Harb, Cairo; tel: 2578 0321/6; www.egyptair.com.eg) is the national carrier for Egypt and operates a network of international services to and from major cities.

From North America, connect to Europe for onward travel to Cairo with Northwest Airlines (www.nwa.com), Air Canada (www.aircanada.ca), Continental Airlines (www.continental.com), Delta Airlines (www.delta.com), American Airlines (www.aa.com) and Virgin Atlantic (www.virgin-atlantic.com).

From Australia and New Zealand you can reach Europe for onward flights to Cairo with Singapore Airlines (www.singaporeair.com), Thai Airways (www.thaiair.com), Qantas (www.qantas.com) and Air New Zealand (www.airnewzealand.co.nz).

By road. The land border with Israel at Rafah (and to a lesser extent Taba in Sinai) has been in use for many years. But be aware that even without an Israeli stamp in your passport, an Egyptian entry stamp at either border will make your passport unusable in some other Arab countries, as this implies entry to/from Israel. The western border with Libya at Sallum is usually open.

By sea. There are daily crossings between Aqaba in Jordan and Nuweiba in southern Sinai: contact the Cairo Navigation Agency, 7 Shari' Abdel Khalek Sarwat, Cairo, tel: 2574 5755/2575 5568.

GUIDES AND TOURS

Larger tour agencies can provide a vehicle, driver and guide for any number of days, whether for Cairo, around the Pyramids of Giza, Saqqarah and Dahshur, the Delta, Upper Egypt, 4x4 driving and camping in the Western Desert, scuba-diving in the Red Sea or trekking in Sinai. Recommended are:

Kimidar Tours: 8 Tersana Sporting Club, Al Muhandesseen, Cairo, tel: 3040 0000, www.kimidartours.com.

MTT (Mediterranean Tours and Travel): 16 Shari' Gawad Hosni, off Shari' Qasr An Nil, Cairo, tel: 2392 0904.

Marhaba Tours: 5a Shari' Ahmed Zeid, Heliopolis, Cairo, tel: 2632 9739, www.marhabatours.com.

Seti First Travel: 16 Shari' Isma'il Muhammad, Zamalik, Cairo, tel: 2736 9829, www.setifirst.com.

Spring Tours: 3 Shari' Al Sayid Al Bakry, Zamalik, Cairo, tel: 2736 5972, www.springtours.com.

H

HEALTH AND MEDICAL CARE

For tourists most sicknesses are temporary, seldom lasting more than 24 hours, being the result of poor hygiene, unclean water or change of environment. Too much sun can cause problems, so always wear a sunhat, sunglasses and use sun cream. Make sure you have full travel insurance and take the following precautions:

- Drink plenty of bottled water and always carry a supply with you. Do not drink tap water and avoid ice in drinks.
- Do not drink the Nile water, swim in it, or walk barefoot along its banks: the water contains bilharzia, a parasitic flatworm.
- Go easy on alcohol, as this will increase the effects of dehydration.
- Wash your hands before eating.
- Eat well-cooked meat and peel fruit before eating it.
- If you eat at buffets, ensure that cold dishes have been well chilled and hot dishes have been freshly cooked.
- Be aware that milk and dairy products may be unpasteurised in non-tourist establishments.

Vaccinations. Nothing compulsory, but polio, tetanus, typhoid and hepatitis A are recommended. Check with your doctor before travelling or online at www.mdtravelhealth.com. Rabies is present in Egypt, so be wary of animals.

For less serious ailments, pharmacies are good places to get quick, professional advice and medicines. Hotels can always call for an English-speaking doctor or locate an open pharmacy.

There are very good hospitals in Cairo, some of which accept credit cards whilst others require payment in cash. These costs are then reclaimed from your travel insurance policy. Anglo-American Hospital Zohoreya, beside the Cairo Tower, Zamalik (tel: 2341 8630); As Salam International Hospital, Korneash An Nil, Al Ma'adi (tel: 2363 8050).

Water. Always drink bottled water, which is cheap and available everywhere. A large bottle of water will cost around 5LE, but hotels and restaurants charge more.

L

LANGUAGE

Arabic is the official language, with Egyptian Arabic widely understood throughout Arab countries from Egyptian television, cinema and music. Even a few words of Arabic will be appreciated by the locals. Some useful Arabic words and phrases:

yes/no	aywa/la
hello	salam aleykum
(response to hello)	aleykum salam
hello/welcome	ahlan wa sahlan
OK	tamam, maashi
please	min fadlak
thank you	shukran
(response to thank you)	afwan
how are you? (to a male)	izayak?
how are you? (to a female)	izayik?
I am fine	Al humdillilah
good morning	sabah Al kher

good evening	mesa Al kher
goodbye	ma'a salama
what is your name?	izmak eh?
my name is….	izmi…
I do not understand	ana mush fahem
do you speak English?	inta bititkalem inglizi?
market	souq
museum	mat haf
mosque	jama
thank God	il-hamdu li-lah

M

MAPS

Reasonable maps of greater Cairo are available outside Egypt. The most detailed is the 1:13,000 published in Hungary by Cartographia, ISBN 978-963-353-157-0, www.cartographiaonline.com. Street names are on the reverse, but confusingly it already shows metro line 3 as being completed. It is also available in the UK from Stanfords in London, www.stanfords.co.uk.

The Cairo Tourist Map by Lehnert and Landrock (their shop is opposite the Egyptian Museum) is a detailed street map of central Cairo.

MEDIA

The Egyptian Gazette (www.egyptiangazette.net.eg), established in 1880, is published daily with a useful listings section of live music, concerts, exhibitions, film shows and cinema. The Saturday version is called *The Egyptian Mail*. Published every Thursday is *Al Ahram Weekly* (http://weekly.ahram.org.eg), an English-language version of the respected, state-owned Arabic newspaper *Al Ahram*. Published in Cairo, the monthly magazine *Egypt Today* (www.egypttoday.com) has interesting local articles and restaurant guides.

Television channels 1 and 2 are national, with English news nightly on Channel 2. Channel 3 is the local Cairo channel, with Nile TV and Dream TV providing imported English programmes. Satellite and cable TV offer greater choice. On the radio are the BBC World Service and English news at FM95.

MONEY

Most of the economy operates on Egyptian Pound (LE) cash, and you should follow suit. Outside top-class hotels and restaurants, bills will need to be paid with cash, not credit cards. Bring US dollars, euros or sterling cash to exchange more quickly at bureaux rather than banks. Traveller's cheques are now a hassle to change, with large commissions charged for doing so. Check before arriving that your card can obtain local cash from one of the many ATMs around Cairo. There are notes for 100, 50, 20, 10, 5 and 1 LE and 50 and 25 piastres (100 piastres = 1LE). There are 1LE coins.

O

OPENING TIMES

Banks. 8.30am–2pm, closed Friday, Saturday and most holidays.
Business. 8am–4/5pm, closed Friday, some on Saturday, and most holidays.
Government offices. 8am–3pm, closed Friday and most holidays.
Shops. 9am–10pm in summer (10am–9pm in winter), often closed Sunday. Government shops are closed 2–5pm for the siesta, and private shops may also close at hours to suit their owners.
Khan Al Khalili bazaar. 10am–9pm, some shops closed Sunday.

P

PHOTOGRAPHY

Take as much memory as you need, as compatible local supplies are uncertain. Ask before taking photos of people, and respect their wishes. Many museums do not allow cameras, and some may charge extra for bringing a camera inside.

| Camera ticket please | **Taskaret kamera min fadlak** |

POLICE

The main police station in Cairo is at 5 Shari' Adly, downtown Cairo. Any tourist in need of help will usually be quickly attended to, with an English-speaking officer nearby. Tourist Police are generally useful, especially those working in the offices at the airport and Rameses Railway Station.

In case of problems, telephone:

| Police: | **122** |
| Tourist Police: | **126** (also Cairo 2390 6028) |

POST OFFICES

The postal system generally works very well, but can be slow. Stamps can be bought from hotels, post offices and some shops. Most post offices are open daily 8.30am–3pm, except Friday and some holidays. The Central Post Office at Meadan Al'Atabah is open 24 hours, except Friday and some holidays. Post overseas mail into blue letterboxes or take it to the post office in person. Allow five days for air mail to Europe and up to two weeks to the US.

PUBLIC HOLIDAYS

There are two types of official holidays when government offices and banks are closed: secular (fixed) and religious (variable dates). Islamic dates move forward roughly 11 days every year with the Islamic calendar.

Fixed holidays

| 7 January | Coptic Christmas |
| 22 February | Union Day |

25 April	Sinai Liberation Day
1 May	Labour Day
18 June	Evacuation Day
1 July	Bank Holiday
23 July	Revolution Day
11 September	Coptic New Year
6 October	Armed Forces Day
23 October	National Liberation Day
24 October	Suez Victory Day
23 December	Victory Day

Variable holidays

Fatih Muharram	Islamic New Year
Ashura Day	Commemorates the assassination of Hussein
Eid Al Fitr	The Minor Feast; celebrates the end of Ramadan for three days
Eid Al Adha	The Grand Feast; commemorates the sacrifice of Abraham

Moulids (holidays celebrating famous birthdays).

Moulid An Nabi	Prophet Muhammad's birthday; celebrated throughout Cairo and Egypt
Sayyidah Zainab	Muhammad's granddaughter; held behind her tomb/mosque and one of the most crowded and colourful
Sayyedna Al Hussain Ar Rifa'i	held in Cairo at Meadan Salah Addin

R

RELIGION

Islam is the official religion, and roughly 90 percent of the population observe Islamic traditions and practices of the Sunni branch. Tourists wishing to visit the famous mosques, mausoleums and madrasahs should remove their shoes. Avoid entering during the five daily prayer times (which change every day), especially Friday mid-day prayers, the holiest time of the week. At some Islamic sites, such as the Muhammad Ali Mosque inside the Citadel, women dressed inappropriately will be asked to wear a gown that covers bare arms, legs and head.

Muslims fast during the month of Ramadan, refraining from eating and drinking during daylight hours. Many restaurants stay closed during the day or may serve special dishes rather than a full menu. Only tourist hotels and a few restaurants will serve alcohol during this period. At all times of the year, respect Islamic tradition by not drinking alcohol in public, except in tourist-orientated bars and restaurants.

Coptic Christians are the largest minority, who, together with Jews and other Christian sects, are officially free to worship at their own services in churches and synagogues.

T

TELEPHONE

The international code for Egypt is 20. The local code for Cairo is 02. To call other cities in Egypt use the following codes:

Alexandria	03
Al Isma'ileyyah	064
Suez/Hurghada	065
Port Said	066
Al Fayyum	084
Asyut	088
Luxor	095
Aswan	097

Most hotels offer direct-dial services from your room, but better value are the many Central Telephone and Telegraph offices (26 Shari' Ramssis, 8 Shari' Adly and Meadan At Tahrir), which are open

24 hours. There are also many private telephone booths offering fast and reliable connections.

Bring your own mobile, as the two major mobile operators (Vodafone and Mobinil) have their own networks and agreements. If staying for some time, consider buying a local SIM card for cheaper rates on internal and international calls. The dialling codes 010 and 012 denote mobile phones.

TIME ZONES

Egypt is two hours ahead of GMT, and there is summer daylight saving (making it one hour ahead of GMT) from late April to late September. Without any adjustments:

New York	London	**Cairo**	Sydney	Auckland
5am	10am	**noon**	7pm	9pm

TIPPING

Even if you speak no Arabic, one word that you will definitely hear is *baksheesh*. Taxi drivers, entry ticket sellers and lift attendants all want *baksheesh*, even if their service has been abysmal. It can be a shock at first, but a relatively small amount in Western terms is a useful boost to a low family income. After a while, you will know who to tip (the helpful hotel waiter or friendly felucca man) and who not to. Any service charges added to a bill will not include a tip, which should be offered at around 10 percent.

TOILETS

Most of the tourist sites are well equipped with good-quality toilets, maintained by an attendant who appreciates a small tip. Wandering round the city, there is no problem using the toilets of restaurants, coffee shops and hotels. Carrying tissues or toilet paper is always a good idea.

where is the toilet?	**fin Al Hammam?**

TOURIST INFORMATION

There are many Egyptian tourist offices worldwide:

Canada: 1253 McGill College Avenue, Suite 250, Montreal, H3B 2Y5, tel: 514-861 4420/(514) 861 8071, email: eta@total.net.

South Africa: First Floor, Regent Place Building, Mutal Gardens, Gradock Avenue, Rosebank, Johannesburg, tel: 011-880 9602/3.

UK: Egyptian House, 170 Piccadilly, London W1V 9DD, tel: 020-7493 5282/3 or 020-7408 0295, email: tourismegypt@visitegypt. org.uk.

US: 630 Fifth Avenue, Suite 1706, New York, NY 10111, tel: 212-332 2570/956 6439, email: egyptoursp@aol.com. 645 N. Michigan Avenue, Suite 829, Chicago, IL 60611, tel: 312-280 4666. 8383 Wilshire Blvd, Suite 215, Beverly Hills, CA 90211, tel: 323-653 8815, email: egypt@etala.com.

In Cairo: The Cairo Tourist Office, Egyptian Tourist Authority and Ministry of Tourism are all at the same location: Misr Travel Tower, Meadan Al Abbassia, Cairo, tel: 2285 4509 or 2284 1970.

Tourist offices are at the airport (tel: 2266 7475 ext 3640), Rameses Railway Station (tel: 2276 4214), Giza Pyramids (tel: 3385 0259) and Shari' Adly (tel: 2391 3454).

TRANSPORT

Metro. The easiest way of getting around Cairo is the cheap and reliable metro system, with trains every few minutes from 5.30am–midnight. There are only two complete lines at present (1 and 2), but the first five stations of line 3 (green) opened in February 2012. Line 3 should be completed by 2019, eventually connecting western and eastern suburbs, and stretching out to the airport. Line 1 (red) is useful for getting to the Christian sites at Al Matariya and ancient Heliopolis at Ain Shams in the northeast, and Coptic Mar Girgis, Al

Ma'adi and Helwan in the south. Line 2 (yellow) is useful for visiting the Muhammad Ali Palace at Koleyet Al Zeraah in the north, but the Giza metro stations in the southwest are a long way from the pyramids. Tickets are bought from offices near the barriers, but avoid rush hours, when it is very crowded.

Taxis. Official black-and-white taxis parked outside the major hotels charge higher prices than those hailed on the street. Always try to fix a price beforehand, by getting local advice on how much the fare should be. Some drivers shrug their shoulders, saying 'as you like', which always ends in one of the parties feeling aggrieved. Getting the meter switched on is even harder. If you find an honest taxi driver who speaks some English, pay them to wait at your destination (especially if it is the pyramids), or maybe hire them for a full day. For special service, limousine taxis can be hired from Misr Limousine (tel: 2259 9381).

Buses. There is a vast network of bus services, but working out the timetable is not easy. If you don't mind crowds and traffic jams, these two routes could be useful: #400 from the airport to downtown; #800 and #900 from the Mugamma'a Building in Meadan At Tahrir to the pyramids.

Trams. The remains of the tram system run north from Rameses Railway Station towards Heliopolis, then split into six suburban lines.

Trains. Good for getting out of Cairo on excursions to the coast or around the Delta. All trains depart from the main railway station at Meadan Al Ramssis (tel: 2575 3555). Tickets should be purchased at least a day in advance. For security, tourists are not allowed on every service, but you will be advised at the ticket office, or the useful Tourist Police office inside the station.

Shared taxis. Another way to get around the Delta is in large estate cars that run between the major towns and cities. Prices are slightly higher than buses, but they are faster and leave when full. Departure points are always near the coach stations, generally close to Meadan Al Ramssis.

V

VISA AND ENTRY REQUIREMENTS

Tourist and business visas are required by most nationalities, and passports must be valid for a minimum of six months. Some nationalities, including UK and US citizens, can obtain single-entry visas on arrival, which is the easiest, quickest and cheapest way. Single- and multiple-entry visas can be obtained beforehand from an Egyptian embassy or through a specialist visa company. Obtain up-to-date information from any tour agency or visa specialist such as Travcour (www.travcour.com) and www.traveldocs.com.

Passports must be registered with the police within 48 hours, which the hotel will arrange. Most items of tourist baggage will be allowed into Egypt without any problem, but laptops and some digital equipment might be recorded in your passport to ensure they leave when you do. There is a duty-free shop upon arrival at Cairo international airport with a personal allowance of one litre of spirits and two cartons of cigarettes.

W

WEBSITES AND INTERNET CAFÉS

Downtown Cairo has a good selection of internet cafés, but they are sometimes hidden away, so ask at the hotel. There are wifi connections at a few modern coffee shops and inside some hotels, but rates per hour vary greatly.

For tourist information and facts:

www.touregypt.net and **www.egypt.travel** Ministry of Tourism websites

www.egypttourism.org Egyptian Tourist Authority in America

www.al-bab.com/arab/countries/egypt.htm

www.yallabina.com general entertainment information

www.egyptianmuseums.net brief information on all the museums

www.egy.com recollections of old Cairo
For news and topical comments:
www.sis.gov.eg/en Egyptian State Information Service
Official external sites:
www.fco.gov.uk
www.state.gov US State Department website

WOMEN TRAVELLERS

Annoyances and unwanted attention are the main problems faced by women travellers, especially those on their own. There is an unhealthy attitude adopted by some local Egyptian men, who see Western women as potentially easy sexual partners. Very occasionally this can develop from lewd comments to actual physical abuse. For the minimum of hassle, wear long, loose-fitting clothing and avoid non-tourist areas and poorly lit streets at night. If you are having problems with anyone in particular, raising your voice in protest and making nearby people aware will usually diffuse the situation. When travelling on the metro, the first car is normally reserved for women and is often less crowded.

Y

YOUTH HOSTELS

Hostelling International hostels (www.hihostels.com) are in Cairo, Alexandria and Al Isma'ileyyah. The Cairo hostel is a high-rise block on Gazirat Al Roadah, close to the Manyal Palace and open daily 7–10.30am and 1–10pm, 35–50LE per person per night. Booking is recommended, the maximum stay is 14 days and youth hostel membership is required.

The hostel in Alexandria has 202 beds at 32 Shari' Port Said, Shatbi, Raml, tel: 03-592 5459. The youth hostel in Al Isma'ileyyah has 275 beds and overlooks Al Timsah Lake. The Egyptian Youth Hostels Association, 1 Shari' Al Ibrahimy, Garden City, Cairo, tel: 2796 1448/2794 0527, email: eyha@link.net also gives details of a hostel in Al Fayyum.

Recommended Hotels

The top class international chain hotels are fairly standard, but some cater more for business guests than others, particularly in the Garden City and Al Ma'adi. The Garden City area south of Tahrir Square (Meadan At Tahrir) is a relatively tranquil area with large hotels spread along the Corniche, and the views they offer guests over the Nile and city are generally magnificent. In the downtown area, there is certainly a lack of good mid-range hotels, and whilst there are plenty of older hotels with atmospheric colonial appeal, many have just become too dilapidated. Some hotels downtown are recommended, but rooms are of varying standards, so if unhappy with what you are given, check to see if they have better ones. Many groups now choose to stay outside the city centre, but basing yourself on the outskirts in one of these mini-resorts means that you are almost self-contained, as there is little on offer outside, such as local shops or restaurants. When the new Egyptian Museum opens near the pyramids there could be a case for some tourists not needing to travel downtown at all.

As a basic guide the symbols are for a double room with private facilities, air-conditioning, breakfast and government taxes.

$$$$$	over US$250
$$$$	US$125–250
$$$	US$80–125
$$	US$50–80
$	under US$50

CAIRO

DOWNTOWN

Capsis Palace $ *117 Shari' Ramssis, tel: 2575 4219/188.* Refurbished hotel with 60 rooms, all with a/c and TV. Coffee bar and ground-floor restaurant. Front rooms can be noisy with busy traffic, side rooms quieter, but very good value and useful for the nearby main railway station.

Cosmopolitan $$ *Shariʻ Ibn Taʻalab, tel: 2393 6914, mobile: 010 633 2599.* Wonderful old building with antique lift, now showing signs of wear and tear, but in the heart of the city. The 84 large old rooms vary tremendously, but a good one is great value. Situated on a side street off Shariʻ Qasr An Nil, so reasonably quiet. Coffee shop, bar and restaurant.

Fontana $$ *Meadan Ramssis, tel: 2592 2321.* Very close to the main railway station and popular for many years with small tour groups and individuals. Ninety rooms in good central location, with a restaurant on the eighth floor and great views across Meadan Ramssis. The small but welcome rooftop pool is 15m in length.

Grand $$ *17 26th of July Street (Shariʻ 26 Yulyu), tel: 2575 7700/7509,* Large hotel of 100 rooms with imposing frontage looking down Shariʻ Talʻat Harb, with the real entrance around the back. Everything is 1930s style, and good value for such a central location. Try the *Valley of the Kings* restaurant or many other eateries nearby.

Happy City $$ *92c Shariʻ Muhammad Farid, Abdin, tel: 2395 9333/ 222, www.happylifehotel.com (then click on 'Choose a Hotel').* Great value hotel just north of Muhammad Naguib metro station. Has sixty rooms but those on the main road can be noisy. Includes a bar, restaurant and *sheesha* smoking on the roof terrace.

Le Riad Hotel de Charme $$$$$ *114 Shariʻ Al Muʻez Li Dinillah, Khan Al Khalili, tel: 2787 6074/5, www.leriad-hoteldecharme.com.* Classic location for this amazing period renovation of a relatively modern building, just down the street from Bayt As Sehaimi. The 17 suites have been tastefully decorated in Egyptian and Arab styles by owners Youssef and Veronique. Views from the rooftop terrace bring Mamluk architecture within touching distance, with the Khan Al Khalili bazaar just down the street.

Osiris $ *49 Shariʻ Nobar, Bab Al Luqʻ, tel: 2794 5728, mobile: 010 53 11 822, www.hotelosiris.fr.* Small family-run hotel, ideally located to the east of Tahrir Square (Meadan At Tahrir). Located on the 12th floor of a quiet block with rooftop terrace looking across to the Citadel. Only 15 rooms and very popular with independent travellers, so reserve early, especially if you want a room with balcony. Internet and laundry service. Highly recommended and great value. No cards, cash only. Can also arrange airport transfer.

Ramses Hilton $$$$$ *1115 Korneash An Nil, 12344 Cairo, tel: 2577 7444, www.hilton.com.* This hotel dominates the Corniche, and is set behind the Egyptian Museum. Fabulous views of the Nile and Giza Pyramids from the 36th-floor rooftop restaurant *Windows on the World*. Pool, terrace, health club and nearby Galleria shopping and entertainment centre. The older, neighbouring Nile Hilton has another 11 restaurants and a casino, but is now looking its age.

GARDEN CITY

Four Seasons Nile Plaza $$$$$ *1089 Korneash An Nil, Garden City, 11519 Cairo, tel: 2791 7000, www.fourseasons.com.* Certainly one of the most luxurious and sumptuous hotels in Cairo, it is part of the exclusive Nile Plaza, with everything for the business and leisure visitor and a choice of quality Italian, Chinese, Japanese and Lebanese cuisines. The vast rooms have magnificent views over the Nile or the Pyramids on the other side. Known as the 'Cairo at Nile Plaza' to distinguish it from the other Four Seasons hotel 'Cairo at the First Residence' located across the other side of the Nile, near the zoo. 365 rooms.

Garden City House $ *23, Shari' Kamal Addin Sala, Garden City, tel: 2794 8400.* This pleasant, if slightly dusty, *pension* is popular with scholars and archaeologists. It has good-sized, clean rooms, is very good value for money, and next door to the Semiramis InterContinental.

Grand Hyatt $$$$$ *Korneash An Nil, Garden City, Al Roadah, tel: 2365 1234, www.cairo.grand.hyatt.com.* Securely located at the northern end of Al Roadah, the views along the Nile from all 716 rooms are superb. All business and leisure facilities you would expect. A choice of 12 restaurants cater for all tastes, and include a revolving restaurant on the 40th floor with stunning views.

Kempinski $$$$ *12 Shari' Ahmed Ragheb, Garden City, tel: 2798 0000, www.kempinski.com/cairo.* New addition to the luxury hotels in the Garden City area. Some rooms with Nile views are available with upgrade. Quality cuisine at *Osmanly* and *Shistawi* restaurants. Wonderful city views from the rooftop pool and Jazz Bar.

Semiramis InterContinental $$$$$ *Korneash An Nil, PO Box 60, 11511 Cairo, tel: 2795 7171, www.intercontinental.com.* In the heart of downtown Cairo, not far from the Egyptian Museum, with facilities including a swimming pool, pharmacy, bookshop, art gallery, beauty salon and lively nightclub. Serves Italian, Lebanese, Thai and French cuisine. Over 800 rooms in one of the largest buildings on the banks of the Nile.

Shepheard $$$$ *Korneash An Nil, Garden City, tel: 2792 1000, www.shepheard-hotel.com.* Not the original Shepheard's Hotel, but a large Nileside hotel that is Egyptian owned and run. Choose from Asian restaurants specialising in Indian, Chinese, Japanese, Thai or Middle Eastern food. Includes a bar, disco and gambling casino. Half of the 298 rooms have Nile views.

ZAMALIK/AL GAZIRAH

Cairo Marriott Hotel $$$$$ *16 Shari' Saraya Al Gazirah, Zamalik, tel: 2728 3000, www.marriott.com.* Almost 1,000 rooms spread over 20 floors located on the former site of Ismail Pasha's Gazirah Palace. Everything as expected in a top-class international hotel, including film theatre, casino and piano bar. Has Italian, Japanese, Middle Eastern and American restaurants.

Hotel Longchamps $$ *21 Shari' Isma'il Muhammad, Zamalik, tel: 2735 2311/2, www.hotellongchamps.com.* Well-located right in the middle of leafy Zamalik, close to many lively shops, bars and restaurants. Occupies the top two floors of an apartment building with a garden terrace. Airport pickup can be provided.

Nile Zamalik $$ *21 Shari' Aziz Abaza, Meadan Sidqy, Zamalik, tel: 2735 1846/2736 3197.* Spread over four floors, set back one block from the Nile, above the Korean Restaurant in a quiet residential area of embassies and old mansions. Slightly old feel and fittings, but very good value considering its location.

Sofitel Al Gezirah $$$$$ *3 Shari' Al Thawra Council, Al Orman, tel: 2737 3737, www.accorhotels.com.* Situated at the very southern end of Al Gazirah island, in quiet and beautiful surroundings near the Opera House. Reasonably close to everything downtown, but confusingly still called by its former name of Sheraton Gezirah by many locals. Another branch of the Sofitel chain called Le Sphinx is located close to the pyramids.

GIZA

Cataract Pyramids Resort $$$ *Al Haraneya, Saqqarah Road, Giza, tel: 3771 8060/1/2, www.cataracthotels.com.* Large complex of villas totalling 383 rooms, set in pleasant gardens around a huge swimming pool. Located south of the Giza Pyramids along the road to Saqqarah, this is a popular local resort in the midst of lush countryside, with its own health club and disco. For a daily fee, the pool can be used by non-residents.

Europa $ *300 Pyramids Road (Shari' Al Ahram), Giza, tel: 3779 5940.* An older style concrete block with 240 rooms over eight floors. Popular with groups and great value, considering the location. Restaurant on ground floor.

Gawharet Alahram Hotel $$ *103 Pyramids Road (Shari' Al Ahram), Giza, tel: 3771 7111, www.gawharetalahramhotel.com.* Also known as the Husa Pyramids Hotel, this is a Spanish-run hotel with 100 rooms and a swimming pool. Wonderful pyramid views from the *Panorama* bar and restaurant on the top floor.

Mena House Oberoi $$$$$ *Pyramids Road (Shari' Al Ahram), Giza, tel: 2377 3222, www.oberoihotels.com.* A former palace of Khedive Ismail, built in 1869 at the foot of the Great Pyramid. It has played host to many famous guests and even been part of Egypt's history when the peace treaty with Israel was signed here in 1979. The newer rooms, built around a beautiful, peaceful garden, have less charm, and the pyramids are slightly further away. Facilities include a swimming pool and several restaurants, including the *Moghul Room*, possibly the best Indian restaurant in Cairo.

Middle East $$$ *85 King Faisal Road, Pyramids, tel: 3740 6061, www.middleeasthotel.com.eg.* Eighty large rooms spread over five floors. Situated on a busy street but good value, only ten minutes from the pyramids, and with a rooftop terrace.

Mövenpick Resort Cairo-Pyramids $$$$ *Alexandria Road, Pyramids, tel: 3377 2555/2666, www. moevenpick-cairo-pyramids.com.* One of several international chains with hotels close to the pyramids, offering floodlit tennis courts and 270 bungalow-style rooms offering glimpses of the pyramids. Popular with groups. A larger Mövenpick resort is located beyond the pyramids, close to the Media City Studios and the Magic Land amusement park.

Pyramid View $ *Nazlet Al Samman, 9 Shari' Abo Al Hool, Giza, tel: 3384 5968, mobile: 010 519 7669, rahomafayed@hotmail.com.* Not to be confused with the larger hotel of the same name on the main Pyramids Road. Simply furnished in 2005 by owner Rahoma Kamel Fayed, there are only six small, clean rooms in this family-run establishment on the doorstep of the Sphinx and pyramids. Has great rooftop views. Only breakfast served but many local restaurants nearby.

Pyramisa $$$$ *60 Shari' Giza, Ad Duqqi, tel: 3336 7000/8000/9000, www.pyramisaegypt.com.* Large 11-floor building with 377 rooms on the west bank of the Nile, opposite the northern end of Al Roadah Island. Italian, Chinese and Egyptian restaurants, gambling casino, two swimming pools, gym and piano bar. Popular with tour groups.

Sheraton Cairo Towers $$$$ *Meadan Gala, Giza, tel: 3336 9700/800, www.sheraton.com/cairo.* 650 rooms with Nile or Giza views and seven dining facilities to choose from, including *Casablanca* on the 26th floor, overlooking the Nile. Contains a health club, swimming pool and gambling casino. Located just west across the Gala'a Bridge (Kubri Gala'a) beyond the southern end of Al Gazirah Island.

AL MA'ADI

Sofitel Cairo Maadi Towers & Casino $$$$$ *Korneash An Nil, Al Ma'adi, tel: 2525 0601/2, www.accorhotels.com.* Overlooking the Nile

12km (7 miles) south of downtown, with distant views to the pyramids. Has 173 rooms, business centre, ballroom, casino and heated pool.

Villa Belle Epoque $$$$$ *Road 13, Villa 63, Al Ma'adi, tel: 2358 0265/2991, www.villabelleepoque.* This luxury boutique hotel perfectly evokes the 1920s Nileside era of Agatha Christie and Howard Carter. Each of the 13 rooms in the period building has a terrace or conservatory and has been individually decorated by owners Tarek and Beryl. Superb meals served upon request, inside or out in the leafy, lush garden. A felucca trip can be taken from their private access point beside the nearby Nile. The same owners also run the period cruise boats MS *Eugenie* and MS *Kasr Ibrim* on Lake Nasser and a fleet of luxury *dahabiyya* sailboats on the Nile in Upper Egypt.

HELIOPOLIS

The Karvin $$ *11 Shari' Muhammad Ebeid, Meadan Al Saba'a Emarat, Heliopolis, tel: 2690 6453, www.thekarvinhotel.com.* Great little hotel midway between the airport and the city centre. Ideal for visiting the locations around Al Matariya connected with the journey of the Holy Family. The Indian restaurant has a deserved high reputation; the rooftop bar and terrace is an oasis of calm.

Le Meridien $$$$ *51 Shari' Al Orouba, Heliopolis, tel: 2290 5055/ 2290 1819, www.lemeridien-heliopolis.com.* Located close to the airport on one of the main roads into the city, with nearby golf course. 283 rooms with all facilities, ideal for the business traveller who also wants to see something of the sights. Another branch of the Meridien chain is located at the pyramids.

AL FAYYUM

Helnan Auberge $$$$$ *Lake Qarun, Al Fayyum, tel: 084-698 1200, www.helnan.com.* Converted former hunting lodge of King Farouk, built in 1937 on the banks of Lake Qarun in the Al Fayyum oasis. 70 rooms set around a swimming pool with gardens, as seen in countless old Egyptian films. Ideal retreat for those wanting to escape the chaos of greater Cairo.

Al Salamlek Palace $$$$$ *Montazah Gardens, Alexandria, tel: 03-547 7999; www.sangiovanni.com.* Built in 1892 as a hunting lodge, this was the palace of King Farouk before his abdication in 1952. An intimate hotel of 20 rooms that manages to make guests feel as if they are part of a house party, the Al Salamlek Palace is totally refurbished, although it still retains many period features. Facilities include a gourmet restaurant, private beach and casino.

Cecil Hotel $$$$$ *16 Meadan Sa'd Zaghlul, 1726 Alexandria, tel: 03-487 7173, www.accorhotels.com.* Situated along the seafront, right in the centre of the city. Built in 1929, this was *the* hotel to stay at when visiting Alexandria, made famous by guests such as Winston Churchill, Noël Coward and Lawrence Durrell, who used it as a location in his *Alexandria Quartet*. Still with its atmospheric bar, but now thoroughly modernised and run by the French hotel chain Accor. 86 rooms.

Windsor Palace $$$ *17 Shari' Ash Shohada Street, Ramleh Station, Alexandria, tel: 03-480 8123/8256, www.paradiseinnegypt.com.* A wonderful old creaking hotel, like its neighbour the Cecil, a couple of blocks away. Of the 76 rooms, side rooms are quieter. Sea views cost extra, but cars along the Corniche dragstrip can be noisy. Part of the Paradise Inn Group, which also run the Paradise Inn Beach Resort and Le Metropole Hotel in the city.

Mercure Accor $$$$ *PO Box 77, Al Isma'ileyyah, tel: 064-391 6316, www.mercure.com or www.accorhotels.com.* The main hotel in the city is beautifully situated beside Lake Timsah, which links to the canal, but is often quite empty. Rooms with views across the lake are 20 percent more expensive, but to see the ships transit the canal in the distance is well worthwhile, which you can also do from the lakeside swimming pool. Service taxis offer local sightseeing tours, as well as return trips to Cairo, Suez and Port Said.

INDEX

Berlitz ® pocket guide

Cairo

Second Edition 2012
Reprinted 2013

Written by Chris Bradley
Updated by Chris Bradley
Commissioning Editor: Catherine Dreghorn
Copy-editor: Stephanie Smith
Picture Researcher: Lucy Johnston
Series Editor: Tom Stainer
Production: Tynan Dean, Linton Donaldson and Rebeka Ellam

Photography credits: Chris Bradley/Apa 10, 13, 14, 15, 30, 31, 33, 34, 36, 37, 38, 40, 42, 44, 46, 47, 48, 51, 52, 54, 55, 60, 66, 71, 73, 75, 76, 79, 80, 81, 87, 90, 95; Corbis 3CR, 45, 49, 82, 89, 93, 100, 105; Fotolia 1, 2TR, 3TR, 3BL, 4TL, 4TR, 4BL, 4-5B, 5BC, 8, 29, 63, 69, 96, 103; Glyn Genin/Apa 4TR, 5TL, iStockphoto 2TL, 2CR, 4BC, 5BR, 26, 59, 61, 72, 74, 85, 86, 94, 98, 101; Axel Krause/Apa 17; Lebrecht 57; Mary Evans Picture Library 19, 21, 22, 28; Topham 24

Cover picture: Corbis

Every effort has been made to provide accurate information in this publication, but changes are inevitable. The publisher cannot be responsible for any resulting loss, inconvenience or injury.

Contact us

At Berlitz we strive to keep our guides as accurate and up to date as possible, but if you find anything that has changed, or if you have any suggestions on ways to improve this guide, then we would be delighted to hear from you.

Berlitz Publishing, PO Box 7910, London SE1 1WE, England.
email: berlitz@apaguide.co.uk
www.insightguides.com/berlitz